Lent For Busy People

LENT
FOR BUSY
PEOPLE

edited by

Shelagh Brown

●》 the bible reading fellowship

Text copyright © 1993 BRF

Published by
The Bible Reading Fellowship
Peter's Way
Sandy Lane West
Oxford
OX4 5HG
ISBN 0 7459 2967 2
Albatross Books Pty Ltd
PO Box 320
Sutherland
NSW 2232
Australia
ISBN 0 7324 0896 2

First edition 1993
Reprinted 1994 (twice)

Acknowledgments

Good News Bible copyright © American Bible Society 1966,
1971 and 1976, published by the Bible Societies and Collins.
The Jerusalem Bible copyright © 1966, 1967 and 1968 by
Darton, Longman & Todd Ltd and Doubleday & Company,
Inc.
The *Revised Standard Version* of the Bible, copyright © 1946,
1952, 1971 by the Division of Christian Education of the
National Council of the Churches of Christ in the USA.
The *New Revised Standard Version* of the Bible, copyright ©
1989 by the Division of Christian Education of the National
Council of the Churches of Christ in the USA.
The Holy Bible, *New International Version*, copyright ©
1973, 1978, 1984 by International Bible Society. Used by
permission of Hodder and Stoughton Limited.
New English Bible copyright © 1970 by permission of
Oxford and Cambridge University Presses.
The Holy Bible, *Living Bible Edition*, copyright © Tyndale
House Publishers 1971.
Extracts from the Authorized Version of the Bible (The King
James Bible), rights of which are vested in the Crown, are
reproduced by permission of the Crown's Patentee,
Cambridge University Press

A catalogue record for this book is available
from the British Library
Printed and bound in Great Britain
by Cox and Wyman Ltd.

Cover Photograph Credits:
George Carey: © Derek Tamea
Susan Howatch: © Barbara
Pollard
Cliff Richard: © Sue Andrews
Terry Waite: © Adam Butler/
Press Association Ltd

CONTENTS

INTRODUCTION

O n the 15th October 1993 there were three items in *The Times* about English football hooligans. *Major apologises to Holland for football hooligans* was the headline to a piece by John Goodbody, the sports news correspondent.

'John Major,' he wrote, 'apologised to Ruud Lubbers, the Dutch prime minister, yesterday for this week's hooliganism in Holland during which more than 1,100 English football supporters were arrested. He condemned their behaviour and said it would be discussed by government departments to decide what further action could be taken...'

One of the leading articles was about the same thing—with a sub-heading *British self-esteem receives another foul blow.*

'As a nation's cultural assets dwindle' said the leader writer, 'so the pressure upon its sportsmen to succeed increases. The ignominy of England's exclusion from European club football in the 1980s was perhaps offset by the cachet of other British exports: technology, military excellence, financial services, new theories of markets and the state.

'But today, the national cupboard seems bare or, at best, dusty with mediocrity. Britain is now better known abroad for the horror of its child murders and its football violence than for its economic prosperity, martial prowess and intellectual vigour.

'For a sense of national decline, there are no pat solutions...'

Then, on another page, on another subject, Ruth Gledhill, *The Times* religion correspondent, reported an inaugural lecture by Mary Grey, the new professor of contemporary theology at Southampton University. Professor Grey argued 'that theology has a strong future in a secularised, post-industrial and multi-faith society, and was capable of transforming such a society'. The task of theology, she said, is 'to keep vision alive, in a culture which is short-changed on this, giving us only yet brighter visions of Disneyland as our communal dream for the future.'

Theology and football hooligans don't seem to have much in common. But there is a vital connection. Theology is the study of religious faith, practice and experience, especially the study of God and his relation to the world.

To study the Christian faith is to discover that even the people in Britain involved in 'the horror of its child murders and its football violence' are made 'in the image and likeness of God'. So is every human being in the whole world—whatever they have done.

We have horribly damaged the image and likeness of God in us by our sin—but the Christian faith says that anything can be forgiven, and that God loves the world and every individual in it so much that Christ died for it.

The Christian faith says that God is like Jesus—and that Jesus was the friend of sinners. The 'good' religious leaders of his day criticized him for it. Jesus had just gone to a party that was given by a Jew who collected taxes for the Roman occupiers of the Jewish nation (and paid himself by demanding taxes that were over the odds). '"Why do you eat and drink with tax collectors and sinners?" asked the Pharisees and the teachers of the law.

'Jesus answered them, "It is not the healthy who need a doctor, but the sick. I have not come to call the righteous, but sinners to repentance"' (Luke 5:30–32).

The Christian vision sees people as Jesus saw them and as God sees them. The secular world has a different vision. On the same day as *The Times* carried those reports on football hooligans it also had an advertisement for what it would be offering to its readers on Saturday.

'In tomorrow's Times, drama, sex and violence. This week's news? No, next week's TV.'

Then there was a picture of the new insert, with the title *Vision*. Underneath the picture was the hype.

'You'd expect vision from The Times. Tomorrow you'll also find "Vision": a complete guide to the following week's radio and TV—satellite and cable included . . ..'

A tele–vision of drama, sex and violence. Or the Christian vision of a world that God created and loves, and that can change from hating to loving, from violence to kindness, and from being bad to being good. Christianity really is good news for a bad and beautiful world—and the contributors to this book spell it out.

Good news for sinners, for people in prison, and even for people who have committed murder. Good news for people who have no sense of value and for people who find it hard to believe in God because of what they think that science has said about the world. Good news for the dying—and at the end of the day that will include all of us.

Swift to its close ebbs out life's little day;
Earth's joys grow dim, its glories pass away;
Change and decay in all around I see;
O thou who changest not, abide with me...

That is the second verse of one of the greatest hymns ever written—packed with Christian truth and Christian vision: *Abide with me*—that the football fans (and the hooligans) sing at the Cup Final at Wembley. Most people only know the first verse—but even that verse is a prayer. And if anyone prays it then God will hear and answer.

Abide with me; fast falls the eventide;
The darkness deepens, Lord, with me abide:
When other helpers fail, and comforts flee,
Help of the helpless, O abide with me.

Shelagh Brown
Editor

Note: The prayers with an asterisk after them are by me.
I tell you this simply for the sake of accuracy.

WHERE WE START

L ent is a bit like making a garden. Digging up the soil and the weeds. Putting on manure and fertilizer. Looking at catalogues to decide what seeds to buy and what plants to grow. It is the same process for a window box or a garden or an allotment.

'...the world must be cleaned in the winter,' wrote T.S. Eliot in *Murder in the Cathedral*, 'or we shall have only a sour spring, a parched summer, an empty harvest. Between Christmas and Easter what work shall be done?' We have to prepare the soil that is us—and that is where we start. Some of the soil is dry and exhausted. Too much has been taken out of it and not enough put back in. So we have to let ourselves be renewed and refreshed, and Sister Margaret Magdalen shows us how that can happen. This is the 'inner journey' side of Lent.

But there is also planning to be done for the future. Canon Michael Green encourages us to use Lent in the same way that the early church used it. To prepare ourselves—so that we can share the good news with the world that God created and loves.

Ash Wednesday

Sister Margaret Magdalen

Exodus 3:1-3 (NRSV)

Moses was keeping the flock of his father-in-law Jethro, the priest of Midian; he led his flock beyond the wilderness, and came to Horeb, the mountain of God. There the angel of the Lord appeared to him in a flame of fire out of a bush; he looked, and the bush was blazing, yet it was not consumed. Then Moses said, 'I must turn aside and look at this great sight, and see why the bush is not burned up.'

'When I was thinking about a title for this piece the idea of "Burn Out or Burn In" or "Burn-out and the Burning Bush" came to mind, because burn-out is a malaise that afflicts so many of us who are in any sort of ministry. Whether we are clerical or lay, in the healing ministry, youth workers or charity organizers, whatever our particular form of ministry, we are all in danger of ending up as its victims.

'When Moses saw the burning bush he was doing his ordinary work—looking after his father-in-law's flock. It was there, in that ordinary work, that the Divine communicated with him. I believe that when God wants to speak to us he often takes a fairly commonplace happening and gives it some kind of extraordinary significance. Then we experience him in a deep encounter in which the supernatural breaks through the natural. It is the kind of experience with which many of us can identify.

'Reflecting upon these verses in retreat last week they seemed to take on a new personal meaning for me. I was in the "desert" of retreat—and perhaps because I had been going at 90 miles an hour right up until the minute I started it, I found it very difficult at first to become inwardly still. It felt as though I was wandering in a wilderness. If you look on a map, the distance that Moses must have wandered was vast—he travelled from Midian to Horeb! I, too, was 'wandering' fairly aimlessly—longing for some kind of revitalizing encounter with God.

'As the retreat went on (through its ten days) I became aware that for me, the burning bush was within myself. It was an inner fire that was not consumed—amazingly. And I say amazingly, because I had begun to feel that I was heading for ministry burn-out myself.

'My diary had been crammed for months. I had just met the deadline for a book. And there were endless demands on my time and energies. I felt that being a living sacrament or a sacrament of God's presence was all very well—but I was being gobbled up and devoured by other people's needs to the extinction of my own spiritual life and even of being fully human.

'Then came that persistent and strong urge to turn aside and see the burning bush within—the "inextinguishable blaze" on the mean altar of my heart, the fire within that burns without being consumed. As I did so, an immediate stillness entered into me together with a real sense of consolation.

'That was certainly good news!—to know that however little the fire had been fuelled from my end, it was still blazing—or perhaps flickering would be more accurate. But it was still there. And by descending into those depths and turning aside to look at what was within, I was in touch again with the divine centre. What is more, it was a very rich and nourishing silent encounter.

'The good news for all who are in that situation, and who have reached a similar point of exhaustion through being devoured by others, is that whatever we feel on the surface about being consumed, there is a fire within which is never consumed. That spoke to me of God's utter faithfulness—the way he continues to indwell us, even when our busyness is in danger of quenching the flame of the Spirit within us; when it erodes our prayer time and squeezes out our essential solitude with the Lord.

'To discover our burning bush, we need only withdraw and turn aside—in other words, find God in that fire of love. We don't need to work at it. Sometimes we can make things worse for ourselves by turning prayer into yet more busyness and unnecessarily exhausting work, when it should be restful, re-creative and nourishing.

'There are of course times when we all have to wrestle in prayer and the going is tough. When, however, we are in the state of feeling we are being "got at" by everybody, God longs for us to withdraw and just gaze in awe at his burning bush in our depths. We then experience again the reality of his indwelling and receive anew his strength. *Our* fire will always become consumed and burned out. *His* fire never will.'

A way to reflect

Sit and reflect for a few moments on the passage about the burning bush and take that as your starting point. It may be that as you do that it will help you to get still. Then allow God to take what happened to Moses and use it to reassure you. As St Benedict put in his Rule, 'Never doubt the mercy of God.' He is still at work within.

When we feel dried up we sometimes fear that the Spirit of God has left us and departed. That is not so. In spite of all our negligence, our infidelities and getting our priorities wrong, his mercy is rich. We just need to get in touch with that truth, and with him—knowing that he longs for this even more than we do.

Underneath our surface exhaustion (which can be very severe) we will discover that in our deepest depths, the longing for God is still alive and still very strong. With that reassurance, once more the flame in our hearts will sing in our eyes.

Use the following verses as a prayer:

O Thou who camest from above
The pure, celestial fire to impart,
Kindle a flame of sacred love
On the mean altar of my heart.

There let it for Thy glory burn,
With inextinguishable blaze;
And, trembling, to its source return
In humble prayer and fervent praise.

Yet for most of us that request to 'kindle a flame of holy love' has already been answered. So possibly we need now to be praying, 'Refuel the flame of sacred love that flickers rather feebly on the mean altar of my heart. And let that fire be one with your own inextinguishable, unconsumable fire—your divine presence within.'

Sister Margaret Magdalen

Exodus 3:4–6 (NRSV)

When the Lord saw that [Moses] had turned aside to see, God called to him out of the bush. 'Moses, Moses!' And he said, 'Here I am.' Then he said, 'Come no closer! Remove the sandals from your feet, for the place on which you are standing is holy ground.' He said further, 'I am the God of your father, the God of Abraham, the God of Isaac, and the God of Jacob.' and Moses hid his face, for he was afraid to look at God.

'Yesterday we were realizing that right in the depth of us the longing for God is still there and that it is still strong. But when we get trapped in a whirlpool of demands it can pull us down into great depths of despair. At such times we just don't know *how* to nourish the longing for God there in the heart of us.

'It is all very well for people to say to us, "Don't be a prisoner to other people's expectations." It is often a real dilemma as to which ones to disappoint. The onlooker may think the solution is obvious, and say, "You simply need to get your priorities sorted out!" Maddeningly, the onlooker seems to see it as quite a simple matter—and that makes it even worse. For the dilemma is often a very complex one, and such remarks are unhelpful and disheartening. But making space for *some* stillness is an essential step to recovery from burn-out.

'When we are able to get still (and for me the way in to stillness is usually through Scripture) we discover that our life *is* being lived in the presence of God, even though we may have given scant recognition to that truth. If we are living in his presence, ultimately that will lead to integration with him, which is our desire—that our life should be "hid with Christ in God". Then it is his fire that is burning—not our little fire alone.

'When Moses turned aside to look at the fire, God said to him, "Take off your shoes, for this is holy ground." Once we get there into that stillness it is essential for us to "take off our shoes"—metaphorically speaking. It is as if God says to us, "Now that you are here in the divine presence, alone with me, you can take them off because you won't need them. You aren't going anywhere for a while! Stay here with me. Watch and pray . . ."

'Moses took off his sandals before the burning bush but he wasn't detaching himself from the everyday world that he lived in. His feet were still on the ground, in the ordinary mess and muck of the world. He could still feel the sand between his toes. But in that encounter with God he was so overwhelmingly aware of the holy that he was absolutely riveted. He could not (and nor did he want to) go dashing off to carry on with his usual round of work. That can be true for us, too. When one does get deeply in touch with the centre it is quite hard to return to the surface.

'A withdrawal of that kind, however, is not selfish—we need never feel guilty about it. It is not detached from reality. Our feet are still planted very firmly in the ordinariness of life and in the dust of the world. But although we are in touch with it, and aware of it, we are totally absorbed by our meeting with God, and the wonder of his burning love within.

'We become more deeply aware of God's purging work within us. His fire is burning up everything that disturbs his presence in us. We find ourselves humbled before the glory of God. And as we turn aside for this encounter with the God within, to comtemplate that glory, we are often reduced to tears of penitence—but also of joy. Isaac the Syrian says that, "As soon as we get near to the truth of God our eyes begin to pour out tears." I don't know what happened to Moses. But sometimes when we get near to that burning bush we can only weep. We experience that weeping as the mercy of God. They are healing and humbling tears—which are very re-energizing.

'After such an experience I come away feeling raw—but at the same time there is a flow of spiritual energy which has not been there before. In one sense we can think of those tears as a gift which somehow puts us once more in touch with our true selves. They are tears that water and bring alive what has been parched and dried up in us.

'There are many of us who are so often wandering wearily and, at times, hopelessly in a spiritual desert—clergy, counsellors, healers, organizers, and many others. All our devotion, our energies and our skills are directed to the service of the Lord, but, nevertheless, we lose our way. We can't see any familar landmarks and we don't have any insights. We don't even seem to have any desire for God.

'Yet if, in the midst of all that, we *can* turn aside to our "Horeb", we can be assured in that encounter with God that the bush will not burn out, and that he is inviting us to stand on holy ground and be still in his presence. When we allow that to happen and truly turn aside from all the pressures, we will then want to go on standing there—for it becomes gift and call and commission all in one.

'At other times, it seems to me the burning bush can be more like a charcoal fire—over which Jesus says to us, as he did to Peter, "Do you love me?" And he repeats the question. That can really bring the tears as we recall our failures in love! But, in the end, of course, that is what we shall be asked in judgment. That alone. "Do you love me?" *Our* answer to that will be very personal, but here is how St Augustine tried to express his:

'Ere ever I cried to Thee, Thou, Most Merciful hadst called and sought me that I might find Thee and finding love Thee. Even so I sought and found Thee, O Lord, and desire to love Thee. Increase my desire, bestow Thyself upon me, my God. Yield Thee unto me, see I love Thee but too little; strengthen my love. Let love to Thee alone influence my heart, and let the thought of Thee be all my joy.

St Augustine

A cry from the heart

My faith burns low, my hope burns low;
Only my heart's desire cries out in me
By the deep thunder of its want and woe,
Cries out to Thee.
  Lord, Thou art life, though I be dead;
Love's fire Thou art, however cold I be;
Nor heaven have I, nor place to lay my head,
Nor home, but Thee.

Christina Rossetti

The Revd Dr Michael Green

Acts 11:19–24 (NIV)

Now those who had been scattered by the persecution in connection with Stephen travelled as far as Phoenicia, Cyprus and Antioch, telling the message only to Jews. Some of them, however, men from Cyprus and Cyrene, went to Antioch and began to speak to Greeks also, telling them the good news about the Lord Jesus. The Lord's hand was with them, and a great number of people believed and turned to the Lord.

News of this reached the ears of the church at Jerusalem, and they sent Barnabas to Antioch. When he arrived and saw the evidence of the grace of God, he was glad and encouraged them all to remain true to the Lord with all their hearts. He was a good man, full of the Holy Spirit and faith, and a great number of people were brought to the Lord.

'When Lent began to be observed in the early Church, it was part of the Christian *askesis*, or discipline. The purpose of it wasn't to make people introspective. It was to fashion them into a task force to be useful for the kingdom of God. What I fear is that these days (if we observe it at all) Lent has become too interiorized—all about "Me and my spirituality". What I want to suggest is that as well as being a time for personal reflection and self-examination it could be the Lord's battle school for campaigners.

'I love these two passages for a number of reasons, and one of the most exciting to me is that here are a bunch of people breaking out from the chrysalis of Judaism into the secular city of their day. Antioch was the third biggest city in the empire. Full of prostitution. Full of sailors. A big military establishment there and an enormous business centre. A city of a million people—and it was big business.

'It fascinates me that we have got this example before us as we are moving into an increasingly urbanized world. I know we can't go straight from the page of the New Testament to the current situation. But there are seven things here that are really significant. We'll look at four now and three tomorrow. If Christians in our day were to do what those Christians in Antioch did, then we really would make an impact on our society.

'The first thing is that these characters were laymen. In those days there was no difference between clergy and laymen. *Laos* means people, and *cleros* means your "lot" or your "inheritance". The amazing thing is that God calls all Christians his *laos*, his people, and all Christians his *cleros*. He has inherited us and we are his lot. Amazing!

'These men had been kicked out of house and home. They had followed Stephen, and Jerusalem became too hot to hold them. They were full of Christ—and they went around for him. The fourth-century historian Eusebius said that the good news was spread by Christians going from village to village and from hamlet to hamlet to tell other people about the Lord. That is just what these folk did—laymen so full of Christ and they just couldn't keep quiet about him. If our churches were able to mobilize lay people to be unembarrassed about Jesus it would be a fantastic achievement this Lent.

'The second thing was that the burden of their song was Jesus. "They began to speak to the Greeks also, telling them the good news about the Lord Jesus." A lot of people in the Church don't like us to talk about Jesus. We can talk about anything except him. But he is the only card in our pack and we can't afford to discard him as the joker.

'The third thing was the mutual encouragement that went on. When Barnabas turned up he tried to encourage these people. I suppose he had been sent to check things out by the Jerusalem church. But he immediately realized that there was a work of God going on so he got busy encouraging it. There isn't very much encouraging being done in Church circles today—although there is a lot of caterwauling and complaining. But this lovely man Barnabas looked at what was happening and he thought to himself, "The Lord's at work here." And so he encouraged them. That could be a Lenten challenge for us!

'Fourthly, Barnabas and Paul trained those people for over a year. They must have had training for enquirers about the Christian faith, training for new Christians, training for the leadership of the little home groups and fellowships they belonged to. Probably there was training on how to deal with foreign cults. And certainly training on how to live a holy life in the middle of Antioch. Lent is not the only time for training, but it is an invaluable one.'

Think and pray

Think about *laos*, the body, and *cleros*, God's 'lot'. Think about those early Christians, full of Christ and telling everyone about

Jesus. Think about the ministry of encouragement. Think about the training (or the lack of it) in your church. Then pray... *

The Revd Dr Michael Green

Acts 11:27-30; 13:1-3 (NIV)

During this time some prophets came down from Jerusalem to Antioch. One of them, named Agabus, stood up and through the Spirit predicted that a severe famine would spread over the entire Roman world. (This happened during the reign of Claudius.) The disciples, each according to his ability, decided to provide help for the brothers living in Judea. This they did, sending their gift to the elders by Barnabas and Saul...

...In the church at Antioch there were prophets and teachers: Barnabas, Simeon called Niger, Lucius of Cyrene, Manaen (who had been brought up with Herod the tetrach) and Saul. While they were worshipping the Lord and fasting, the Holy Spirit said, 'Set apart for me Barnabas and Saul for the work to which I have called them.' So after they had fasted and prayed, they placed their hands on them and sent them off.

'The next thing that excites me about those people is that they were so practical. They heard there was going to be a big trouble—a severe famine—down in Jerusalem. So they said, "Let's give—straight away." They didn't have a diocesan stewardship officer trying to squeeze money out of them. They had enough love for the Lord to be really generous: when they heard the needs of their brother and sister Christians they said, "OK! Let's go for it!" This hilarious giving is a mark of the gospel. It reflects God's hilarious giving to us. When people see it, they are amazed. And no church that is generous to the needy round about it is ever going to be short of custom—whatever the local need is. The Jesus way is for a church to pour itself out for a perceived need.

'The other thing that was exciting was the fellowship, and it was very remarkable. It was the thing that Paul and Peter fell out about—that there were Jewish believers and Gentile believers sitting down and eating together. Breaking all the taboos on both sides—and creating what the second- and third-century writers came to call a "third race". Not Jews. Not pagans. But something else. A third way. When people see that quality of fellowship in a church (and the nearest you get to it is on a good night in the pub) then those churches grow.

'Finally, they lived a life that reminded people of Jesus. We are all going to fail—but if there is a love for Jesus in us that is transparent, then it really does have an effect. It was those people in Antioch who were first called *Christianoi*. Because they were full of Christ, and it showed, it was the pagans who called them after Jesus.'

Pray

Pray for the needs around you . . . for the fellowship in your church . . . and that you will all live a life that reminds people of Jesus.*

Material for reflection and groups

Let each person tell the others what they are hoping for from these Lent group meetings.

If most people have not read Sister Margaret Magdalen and Canon Michael Green then read aloud one day from each. Talk about the two sides of Lent—an inner journey and also a preparation to share the good news.

Use the prayer suggestions at the end of each day in your final time of prayer and reflection.

GOOD NEWS ABOUT GOD AND ABOUT JESUS

S ome people have such a distorted image of God that I wonder how they can worship him at all. Perhaps they aren't worshipping him. Perhaps they are frightened of him—and simply going to church and going through the motions in case he punishes them for their badness.

The good news is that God is like Jesus—and that we have a Christ-like God. In three days in this section we look at the story which Jesus told us to show us what God is like. We call it the story of the prodigal son. But, as the German theologian Helmut Thielicke once said so beautifully, it is really the story of the waiting father. Waiting for us to come home—and then running out to meet us with his arms wide open.

Week 1 / Sunday

Bishop Richard Harries

Luke 15:11-24 (RSV)

Richard Harries is the Bishop of Oxford and a well-known and popular broadcaster. He almost always does 'Thought for the Day' on BBC Radio 4 on Friday mornings. He has written quite a few books, including *Prayers of Hope*, *Prayers of Grief and Glory*, *Prayer and the Pursuit of Happiness* and *CS Lewis: the man and his God*. At the moment he is working on *A Gallery of Christmas Reflections* for the BRF—with full colour pictures that he has chosen and reflected on.

There was a man who had two sons; and the younger of them said to his father, 'Father, give me the share of property that falls to me.' And he divided his living between them. Not many days later, the younger son gathered all he had and took his journey into a far country, and there he squandered his property in loose living. And when he had spent everything, a great famine arose in that country, and he began to be in want. So he went and joined himself to one of the citizens of that country, who sent him into his fields to feed swine. And he would gladly have fed on the pods that the swine ate; and no one gave him anything. But when he came to himself he said, 'How many of my father's hired servants have bread enough and to spare, but I perish here with hunger! I will arise and go to my father, and I will say to him, "Father, I have sinned against heaven and before you; I am no longer worthy to be called your son; treat me as one of your hired servants."' And he arose and came to his father. But while he was yet at a distance, his father saw him and had compassion, and ran and embraced him and kissed him. And the son said to him, 'Father, I have sinned against heaven and before you; I am no longer worthy to be called your son.' But the father said to his servants, 'Bring quickly the best robe, and put it on him; and put a ring on his hand, and shoes on his feet; and bring the fatted calf and kill it, and let us eat and make merry; for this my son was dead, and is alive again; he was lost, and is found.' And they began to make merry.

'There are so many marvellous passages in the Bible that it's very difficult to choose one of them. I'm not a person who thinks that you have to ram the Bible down people's throats. It stands on its own feet and communicates its own truth. But in the end I wanted something in the Gospels, and it is in the parables that we get such a clear indication of the mind of Christ, conveyed in such a vivid and creative way. I find the parables quite superb. They are always teasing one and questioning one and exciting the imagination. There are always new things in them, and it is very difficult to know which one to choose. But I've chosen the parable of the prodigal son.

'This parable like others says wonderful things about God. They may appear over-simple and hackneyed. But they have a profound simplicity about them. They say that God is a loving God. He is a God who takes the initiative to come towards us, and a God who forgives us. In this parable the father sees the prodigal son coming from a distance and he goes out to meet him—and there's no doubt about it that it is meant to be a picture of the heavenly Father, who was actually made manifest in the ministry of Christ himself in the way that he went out to people who were on the edge of society and people who were wretched. I think this is another reason why the parable is so important: there is such continuity between what is depicted there in such a vivid, pictorial way and the actual ministry of Christ himself. Christ manifested, in his actual ministry, a God who goes out to people, and when this parable talks about the Father it's telling us of a Father who comes to us in his Son.'

A meditation

Think of yourself as the prodigal son, almost at home, and having worked out what you are going to say when you get there—then suddenly seeing the Father running out to meet you with his arms wide open. Then think of yourself as the Father, and imagine your delight when you see your son coming home.*

Bishop Richard Harries

Luke 15:25-32 (RSV)

Now his elder son was in the field; and as he came and drew near to the house, he heard music and dancing. And he called one of the servants and asked what this meant. And he said to him, 'Your brother has come, and your father has killed the fatted calf, because he has received him safe and sound.' But he was angry and refused to go in. His father came out and entreated him, but he answered his father, 'Lo, these many years I have served you, and I never disobeyed your command; yet you never gave me a kid, that I might make merry with my friends. But when this son of yours came, who has devoured your living with harlots, you killed for him the fatted calf!' And he said to him, 'Son, you are always with me, and all that is mine is yours. It was fitting to make merry and be glad, for this your brother was dead, and is alive; he was lost, and is found.'

'It may be that this parable ought to be called the parable of the two sons, or the parable of the elder brother. Most modern scholarship suggests that the parables make one, main, challenging point. They are not allegories, where there are a whole series of bits and pieces of symbolism where one thing stands for another thing. They make one main, thrusting point, and the main thrust of this parable is probably not the father embracing the prodigal son but what the father says to the elder brother who remained at home.

'I find this bit of the parable very important, because it is speaking not only to the Jews at the time of Christ who were unwilling to receive his ministry but to all of us. There is a bit in every one of us which is the elder brother—the resentful one, the up-tight one, the one who stands on his dignity, the one who wants his rights. There is that elder brother in all of us. And I find the words of the father to the elder brother just as moving as the words to the prodigal son, because he says to him, "Son, you are always with me, and all that is mine is yours." You are *always* with me, and it is a question of us realizing that.

'I think the words of the father to the elder brother are particularly appropriate to church people, because those of us who go to church Sunday by Sunday and who try to maintain our church life are in the position of the elder brother. We have stayed at home. We have done our duty. We've done what we're meant to have done—and for that reason it's very easy for us to be resentful or jealous. At the level of the local congregation, when newcomers come in who've had nothing to do with the church, there's often quite a lot of resentment by church people, particularly the inner ruling cliques in congregations. So it applies here and now at the local level but I think it will apply even more in heaven.

'I have no doubt that a great number of people who are not churchgoers will get there before me, and what is my attitude going to be? Is it going to be that of the elder brother? Well, if it is, or if it's likely to be, I need to have those words ringing in my ears: "Son, you are always with me, and all that is mine is yours." I've not lost out on anything if they get there as well, or if they get there before me, because God has been with me all through this life and if I want it he will continue to be with me through the next life.

'So if I went on a desert island and just had to take one passage with me I'd take this passage. It would be very important for the two points of view, because both these sons, the so-called prodigal son and the elder brother, are part of me. Sometimes I will want to be reassured that the Father is there reaching out to me, a person who's gone off to some far country in myself—in sulkiness, or bolshiness, or general giving-upness, or whatever . . . and when I come to my right mind—come to my senses—I need to know that I haven't been totally abandoned. But also the elder brother side of me, the kind of respectable citizen, the more up-tight side, needs both to be confronted and to be assured that I haven't lost anything by doing my duty, because God is with me there. "Son, you are always with me, and all that is mine is yours." For me that means the presence of God, now and hereafter, and all that God has to offer—the gift of life, and the gift of eternal life.'

A way to meditate

I suggest that you should simply be still and become aware of your surroundings—the chair you are sitting on, the table ... and realize that those things only exist because they are held in existence by the power of being which is God himself. If he did not hold them in being then they would simply not be. Those individual entities in their very essence actually tell us something about God—or, rather, something of God is manifested to us through them.

I wrote a prayer once when I was kneeling in church, where God came across to me as the essence of everything that surrounded me: the voice in my voice ... the listening in those who hear ... the heart of the stone ... the sheen of the silver ... or whatever it might be. All inadequate words, but trying to convey the sense that in some way God is in and through all things, as well as the source of all things.

That is not pantheism—it is quite the opposite. God can only be in all things because he is also totally other than all things. It is because he is totally transcendent that he is also able to focus his presence for us in particular ways. He is not tied or limited by anything finite, not even the world itself, and it is because he is utterly other than the world that he can make himself known in and through the world.

The Revd Gerard W. Hughes

John 4:7–11 (JB)

Gerard Hughes is an internationally popular speaker and writer on the theme of spirituality. He wrote the best-selling and much loved *God of Surprises* and, more recently, *Oh God, Why? A journey through Lent for bruised pilgrims* for the Bible Reading Fellowship. He has brought the Ignatian method of prayer right up to date so that ordinary people can use the spiritual exercises, and he shows people how to pray the Bible in a unique way, so that the stories enter into us and come alive within us.

When a Samaritan woman came to draw water, Jesus said to her, 'Give me a drink' ... The Samaritan woman said to him, 'What? You are a Jew and you ask me, a Samaritan, for a drink?' . . . Jesus replied: 'If you only knew what God is offering and who it is that is saying to you: Give me a drink, you would have been the one to ask, and he would have given you living water.' 'You have no bucket, sir,' she answered, 'and the well is deep.'

' "You have no bucket, sir, and the well is deep," is one of my favourite verses in the Gospels for its humour and its depth.

'Jesus sits tired and thirsty at Jacob's well in Samaria. For the Jews, Samaritans were worse than pagans. No self-respecting Jew would have anything to do with a Samaritan: least of all would a Jewish man address a Samaritan woman. Jesus' attitude is the first thing to ponder in this passage.

'God, in Jesus, is no respecter of persons. God addresses every human being, irrespective of race, colour, religion or lack of it, for it is in God that we live and have our being. Hence the saying, "Whenever you meet another person, take off your shoes, for you are entering holy ground. And tread warily, for God has been there before you."

'From the woman's point of view, her answer, "You have no bucket, sir," is perfectly reasonable, but addressed to Jesus the reply is ridiculous. And this is another point to ponder and pray.

'Plato, in his *Republic*, has a wonderful description of our human state. He imagines a cave, and we are all facing the wall. Behind us is a fire, and between us and the fire someone is throwing shadows on the cave wall. We see only the shadows, and consider them to be the whole of reality. The philosophers' task, Plato believed, was to deliver human beings from the shadows and lead them out into the real world. Jesus came to deliver us from darkness into the light.

'In various ways, we keep on saying to God, "You have no bucket, sir." A sense of guilt, for example, blights the lives of many Christians, who feel they cannot be forgiven. Their guilt is real, just as the shadows on the cave wall are real, but the guilt, like the shadow, is not the whole of reality. There is a reality beyond guilt, the reality of God's love and forgiveness, always greater than we can ever think or imagine. What matters most of all is that we should allow that love and forgiveness into our own lives, then let it flow through to all those we meet. It is in our relationships with ourselves and with others that we meet God.

'Recently, an Anglican vicar declared that he does not believe in God, which has opened up the God debate again. Whoever denies God is saying, "You do not match up to the criteria which I have set down if you are to qualify as God," which is to repeat the woman's phrase, "You have no bucket, sir." '

A prayer

God, your existence is beyond the reality I experience, so, in that sense, you do not exist as I know existence, or as a bucket exists. But your Spirit is within us and our hearts can glimpse what our minds cannot comprehend.

To our minds and senses you are invisible, intangible, imperceptive, a void, no-thing.

To our hearts you are a longing, a yearning, a desiring for we know not what, and in that emptiness you show yourself in a knowing which is also a not-knowing.

You are delicate, powerless, vulnerable. I think you are shy. Yet you are in all things, renewing all things, vibrant in every atom, closer to me than I am to myself, leading me out of the shadows into the reality that is You.

Give me a still heart which can recognize the beauty of your face in the dark and frightening shadows of our lives.

Cliff Richard

Galatians 3:26-28 (RSV)

When someone is as well known as Cliff Richard there isn't much you need to say about them. One of the most popular singers there has ever been, Cliff has been pulling in the crowds for over thirty years. Singing brilliant songs that head right up to the top of the charts and win him gold discs: 'Living Doll' and 'We don't talk any more' are just two of them. Cliff also sings about his Christian faith—and writes about it: *The Way I See It Now* in 1975, and *Jesus, Me and You* in 1985. He gave me an interview in his room at the theatre—relaxed, easy and with a lot of charisma. He read out the Bible passage he had chosen and started to talk to me about it.

For in Christ Jesus you are all sons of God, through faith. For as many of you as were baptized into Christ have put on Christ. There is neither Jew nor Greek, there is neither slave nor free, there is neither male nor female; for you are all one in Christ Jesus.

26

'I love this, because it tells everyone exactly what a Christian is. You put on Jesus, and Jesus becomes you. He becomes an integral part of your life. And when that's happened it means there is no black or white. There should be no apartheid. There should be no hate. It even goes so far as to say that even the differentiation between male and female is stopped.'

At this point Cliff and I had a small argument, since I don't believe that the new creation is unisex. I was sure he didn't believe that either, but I wanted to get it clear. 'The bad bit of differentiation is stopped,' I said to him. 'Well, any bit. In God's sight we're now seen as total equals, as one type of person. You and I can face each other as spiritual equals.'

'Yes,' I said, 'but different.'

'Yes, of course, different,' said Cliff. 'Equality's all right—but sameness isn't. One of the things I've loved about Christianity is that it doesn't take away our individuality. In fact God seems to reinstate the individual in you when you become a Christian. I know that I'm far more distinctive a person than I ever was before, and certainly I'm more outspoken.

'However, being unafraid doesn't stop me being upset by things that I read about me—and I've begun to believe that although we're told to turn our other cheek when people say or do things, it doesn't say we can't actually defend and even sometimes attack—though I don't mean in a violent, physical way. So therefore if people ask me my opinion on something I give it to them straight.

'It's like when people say to me, "Do you believe that Christianity is the only way?" The answer is, "I'm sorry if it offends you, but yes, it is the only way—I believe that." I think quite often Christians are guilty of complicating the issue. It's as simple as coming to terms with a few basic questions. "Was there a Jesus?", "Is he the Son of God?", "Did he die for your sins?", "Is he alive now because the resurrection's true?"

'And if you come to the positive and the affirmative on all those, then the next step is to say, "Jesus, I want you in my life"—and that clinches it. So becoming a Christian is saying, however you phrase it, "Jesus, I need you in my life"—and he enters. You've put on Christ.

'But if we put on the mantle of being Christians then we also take on the robe of saying, "I am no greater and no less than anybody else. In God's sight I am saved through Jesus, and equality is something we attain because of that." And you suddenly understand that you are the same as everyone else.

'Look at me, for instance. I have a position that is given great esteem.

When I go out of the stage-door, there are people who've come to look at me and get my autograph—and there's this feeling of "They think I'm wonderful." Perhaps that's why I like this Scripture so much—because it reminds me that I'm just the same as everyone else. I know I have a specific role to play that perhaps is unique. But there are countless other people who do similar work and many who are far more famous! But this is my role—and I have to be aware all the time that in God's sight fame counts for nothing. Somehow I've got to keep that in mind.'

A prayer

God, help me. Continue to open my understanding—so that all the time I can learn more about the practical implications of being 'one in Jesus', and more about how to be equal with people.

Kriss Akabusi

Matthew 11:28-30 (NIV)

Kriss Akabusi is a perfect image for the sub-title of this book. He was bad—and he is beautiful. Bad in that he wasn't faithful to his wife—whom he really loved very much. Beautiful in that he has a perfect body in tip-top physical condition—and a smile that makes you feel that the sun has started to shine.

He was standing in the hotel foyer talking to one of the guests when Richard Fisher (BRF's Chief Executive) and I arrived to have dinner with him. While we were eating, people kept coming up to our table. 'Can I have your autograph for my son?' someone would say. Then (a bit shy at asking for themselves) 'and please can I have one for me as well?'

Kriss was totally unfazed and totally relaxed. He had a stack of photographs printed on cards, with a space at the left hand side for him to write on. There is one of them now on my mantlepiece: 'Shelagh. Keep smiling. Kriss Akabusi.' And every time I look at it I do smile—because of the way he is smiling out of the photograph.

But he doesn't just hand out signed photographs. Along with each one he gives everyone a leaflet. His career summary is on the back of it: 1984 Olympic Silver Medal 4x400m relay; 1986 Commonwealth Gold Medal 4x400m relay. Plus more silver medals and gold medals and two Olympic Bronze Medals for the 400m hurdles and the 4x400m relay.

There is also a short account of the real turning point in his life. This is an extract from it.

'In 1986 [Kriss] was at a crossroads. He was a useful 400m runner but was frankly never going to be world class.

'Two decisions in the next year dramatically changed the direction of his life. He switched events from the 400m to the 400m hurdles, and became a Christian.

'The switch of event was well thought out. Kriss noticed that Britain had a wealth of talent at 400m and that his ranking was dropping. However, there were no outstanding 400m hurdles it seemed. Kriss then embarked on a schedule which would bring him medals at Commonwealth, European and World Championships in the event.

'At the Commonwealth Games in 1986 in Edinburgh, Kriss found a Good News New Testament in his room. He read it from cover to cover during the games. In his own words:

"Of course I had heard about Jesus before, but I had never realized that he had walked on earth and that he had said so many amazing things or that he had promised eternal life to anyone who believed in him. When I realized all these things about him I just knew that I had a decision to make. I started investigating to find out if it was true what he said. A few months later I made a decision to give my life to Jesus Christ, something I have never regretted." '

When we had all finished dinner—and Kriss had finished signing photographs and giving away leaflets—the three of us went to his room so that I could interview him. I wanted him to tell me about one or two Bible passages that were important to him and that fitted in with the theme of good news for a bad and beautiful world.

'The first one that means a lot to me is Matthew 11:28–30,' Kriss said. He turned to it in his Bible and read it out . . .'

Come to me, all you who are weary and burdened, and I will give you rest. Take my yoke upon you and learn from me, for I am gentle and humble in heart, and you wil find rest for your souls. For my yoke is easy and my burden is light.

'When I was a youngster,' Kriss said, 'I grew up in a children's home. And I wanted all the things that my friends had who came from lovely homes. Lovely clothes, cars, and all the material things. I worked very hard for them—and through going into the army and through athletics I became relatively wealthy and I acquired them. I got the sort of car I'd always wanted—a Mercedes Benz. It was a small one—a 1.90—but it was an MB!

'But all those things I had didn't give me the happiness that I wanted. And there was something else. I was married—and I still am. Although I loved her (not knowing what love really was—and I'm still finding out!) I had got used to her. She was everything that I needed for me—but I wasn't faithful to her. She knows that now. But it disturbed me. Why wasn't I faithful? That woman was all I really cared for. But that was all part and parcel of it. I had all the things I wanted but they weren't satisfying me.

'Then we lost some twins. They were stillborn. Because I was wondering where they had gone to I began to ask spiritual questions. Ecclesiastes 7:2 and 4 says that wisdom is found in the house of mourning. And that is exactly right. Because these two loved people died before they lived it got me thinking.

'When I went to the Commonwealth Games in 1986 there was a Good News Bible by my bed. Just the New Testament—and for the first time in my life it was in plain English. I read it all in the two weeks I was there and I met this guy called Jesus. One of the many things he said was "I will give you life in all its fullness." And I loved what Jesus said. But I couldn't really believe that this guy was really real.

'I did lots of reading—reading all sorts of books—and I was really thinking about Jesus. Then I went to America and on April 14 1987 I went to bed feeling very frustrated and saying, "God, if you're really out there—Jesus, if you're really who you say you are—will you just let me know?"

'I went to bed and I had a vision—a vivid dream where I was on a waterbank. I jumped into the water and I was swimming towards the voice that I could hear. It was turbulent water and hard work, and all of a sudden the turbulence turned me around and started taking me with it. I started to lose my confidence. But I kept on going—and all of a sudden I rushed into this giant figure. There was a great big fountain gushing out of the water, and there was a great big figure of Jesus. I just knew it was Jesus—and as I saw him those were the words I heard.

' "Come unto me those who are weary and heavy laden and I will give thee rest. For my yoke is easy and my burden is light." And that was just like "Bang!" As I heard those words I yelled out "Jesus!"

'I sat on my bed and I just thought about Jesus, and I was so peaceful and so tranquil and so happy. I wrote these things all down, then the next morning when I woke up I looked at my filofax and it was all there. Written down. My baptism by the Holy Spirit.

'That morning I went down to the track and I spoke to all the guys. All of a sudden all that factual knowledge that I had went from my head to my heart. All those doubts went away and I was just telling everybody about Jesus. That Scripture opened it up. All of sudden all my burdens, all my hopes, all my fears, and all the things I'd been trying to work for were just answered like that. So that's why that Scripture is very important for me.'

A promise

Come to me, all you who are weary and burdened, and I will give you rest. Take my yoke upon you and learn from me, for I am gentle and humble in heart, and you will find rest for your souls. For my yoke is easy and my burden is light.

Kriss Akabusi

Ecclesiastes 7:24; Proverbs 9:10 (NIV)

Whatever wisdom may be, it is far off and most profound—who can discover it?

The fear of the Lord is the beginning of wisdom, and knowledge of the Holy One is understanding.

'I have got a private number plate: ECC 724', Kriss told me. I grinned 'Nice to be rich!' Kriss grinned as well. 'Yes. And ECC 724 has got a dual meaning for me: Ecclesiastes 7:24 plus 7:2 and 7:4. The first one is this.

' "Wisdom. What is it? It's hard to find and who can know it?" It's a great question. We are constantly bombarded with different ideas of what wisdom is. When I was at school the age of the earth went from something like 60 million years to 25 million years. And I was only there five years! I don't know what the answer is. We men are so wise and yet so limited.

'And the question is, "What is it all about? Where are we going? Where did we come from? Is there a God?" These are all matters of wisdom. The answer the Bible gives is Proverbs 9:10. "The fear of the Lord is the beginning of wisdom…" What that means to me is that wisdom is knowing why you do what you do. What is the motivating factor for what you do? Considering the end of all things before you begin.

'If you have a philosophy that "this is it, and this is all of it, and that what we are experiencing now is what it is," then your particular sort of wisdom—conventional wisdom—is, "Grab what you can and do what you can while you can. The end justifies the means." In that sort of scenario it's not crime that's wrong. It's getting caught.

'But what the Bible has taught me is that the fear of the Lord is the beginning of wisdom. That's not to say that I shake every time I think of God. But it's the knowledge that God is watching us. God is watching you and watching me. God has got a plan for my life and for your life—and there is a reason for living.

'There is more to life than meets the eye. It isn't just that I was born and I will die and after death there is no life. There is something else. And for me the realization that all I see and touch and feel in this world is just a small part of eternity has really changed the whole direction of my lifestyle.

'Then when Monica's grandma died I was going through the Bible and I looked at Ecclesiastes 7:2 and 7:4. (This is the dual meaning of 7:24 for me.) 7:2 says "It is better to go to a house of mourning than to go to a house of feasting, for death is the destiny of every man; the living should take this to heart." And 7:4 says, "The heart of the wise is in the house of mourning, but the heart of fools is in the house of pleasure."

'I don't know about you, but I think God is wonderful! God gave me this question: Ecclesiastes 7:24. "What is wisdom? It is most profound. It is hard to find." And traditionally Proverbs 9:10 is the answer. But here in Ecclesiastes 7:2 and 4 God tells me that if you think about the end you realize that as you are born so you are going to die.

'When you start to put things in context you realize the fragility of life. There is wisdom. It's realizing that God is the answer. That the beginning of wisdom is just the fear of God. I enjoy life. I'm a happy-go-lucky guy. I also know that this temporal thing is going to end. But there is something else afterwards.'

A promise

If any of you lacks wisdom, he should ask God, who gives generously to all without finding fault, and it will be given to him.

James 1:5 (NIV)

Bishop Michael Marshall

Luke 15:17–21 (NIV)

Bishop Michael Marshall (together with Michael Green) is one of the Archbishops' Advisers on Evangelism. A popular broadcaster and writer, he travels widely in Britain and abroad to speak and teach in connection with Springboard, which is the Archbishops' Initiative on Evangelism. His books include *Glory under your Feet*, *The Freedom of Holiness* and (published by the BRF) *Expectations for Evangelism*.

When he came to his senses, he said, 'How many of my father's hired men have food to spare, and here I am starving to death! I will set out and go back to my father and say to him: Father, I have sinned against heaven and against you. I am no longer worthy to be called your son; make me like one of your hired men.' So he got up and went to his father. But while he was still a long way off, his father saw him and was filled with compassion for him; he ran to his son, threw his arms around him and kissed him. The son said to him, 'Father, I have sinned against heaven and against you. I am no longer worthy to be called your son.'

'About a year ago a priest burst into tears as I gave him his communion. It was at a clergy conference in Canterbury, and afterwards I sought him out. He talked to me about his father, whom I knew was a brilliant mathematician. I shall never forget one thing that he said. "I learned as a little boy that the only way I could get the attention of my father was to be a bad boy." "That's extraordinary," I said to him. "Because I learned that the only way I could get the attention of anybody was to succeed."

'When I was eleven, in my first year in senior school, I was bottom of the class. But the next year I was top—and I never budged from that. I learned in that year that the way to get attention was to be clever and to be good. Good in the rather sickening sense.

'What the prodigal son didn't realize was that it was all right to be a bad son. On his way back to the father he was preparing a little three-point speech. He would have been rehearsing it and refining it in the months or the years that it took him to get back home. Perhaps trying to make out some sort of case for himself and to justify himself. Perhaps thinking, "I'd rather give myself ten out of ten for being a slave than get nil out of ten for being a son."

'But when he gets there he doesn't say that last phrase in his prepared speech—"make me like one of your hired men..." He says to his father, "I have sinned against heaven and against you. I am no longer worthy to be called your son." And that has to be said. We cannot call black white.

'What he had really said to his father before he left home was "I wish you were dead now." I found that out through Ken Berry, who says that in the Middle Eastern world you couldn't ask for your inheritance ahead of time. It only came to you when your father died. So the prodigal was saying to Dad, "I wish you were dead now. I want the inheritance *now*." And in effect the father says, "All right. If you want me dead then to all intents and purposes I'll be dead..."

'In the musical *Godspell* they got what the prodigal said wrong. On the whole, *Godspell* is extremely accurate, but they had the son asking the father to make him like one of his hired men. And I think that points to one of the problems of this generation. It doesn't know how to be a bad son.

'I don't think I have known how to be a bad son. There is a phrase in *The Black Dog* by Anthony Storr where he says that Churchill was like many depressives, who cannot understand how they can be loved. They know how they can impress. And they often want people to look up to them. But they do not know how to be loved just for being themselves—for better or for worse.

'My own father remarried just six months after my mother had died of cancer. I was eighteen, and it was an enormous blow. I went to my stepmother's house for dinner and on the dinner table were things from my mother's home. So that broke down our relationship totally. I think I would be more understanding about that now. But at the time I couldn't handle it. So we really had very little to do with each other.

'Then when I was made a bishop my father sent me a telegram with just the words "Well done, son." Afterwards I said to him: "If only you could have said that to me twenty years earlier..." I wanted to be a pianist—and that had been unacceptable. And when I wanted to be a priest that was totally unacceptable. "No son of mine is going to do that," he said to me, "That's not a real man's job—to be a priest."

'I believe our parents' job is to affirm us and to say "Well done!" to us. We need to hear that many times—and it's an echo of the One we really need to hear it from. Because in the embrace of his father the son was restored in every sense. Henri Nouwen has just written a book about the prodigal son, and on the cover of it is that lovely Rubens painting. You can see the Father's face (but not the boy's) and the hands of the Father round the back of the boy—holding him in his arms in a total embrace.

'The Father had run out to meet him, thrown his arms around him, and kissed him. But in the Middle East an old man would never have run, because if he had he would totally have lost his dignity. Which is just what God did on the cross. He ran to meet us and he lost all his own self dignity. It's what that marvellous passage in Philippians is talking about.'

Let the same mind be in you that was in Christ Jesus, who, though he was in the form of God, did not regard equality with God as something to be exploited, but emptied himself, taking the form of a slave, being born in human likeness. And being found in human form, he humbled himself and became obedient to the point of death—even death on a cross.

Philippians 2:5–8 (NRSV)

A prayer

Father of all, we give you thanks and praise, that when we were still far off you met us in your Son and brought us home. Dying and living, he declared your love, gave us grace, and opened the gate of glory. May we who share Christ's body live his risen life; we who drink his cup bring life to others; we whom the Spirit lights give light to the world. Keep us firm in the hope you have set before us, so we and all your children shall be free, and the whole earth live to praise your name; through Christ our Lord. Amen.

Material for reflection and groups

Ask each person to say what is their own image of God.

Read out either Bishop Michael Marshall's or Bishop Richard Harries' (first) piece. Talk about whether you need to change your ideas about God in view of what Jesus said.

Finish by using the way to meditate at the end of Richard Harries' second piece. Then use Gerard Hughes' final prayer.

GOOD NEWS TO THE OPPRESSED AND RELEASE TO THE PRISONERS

I f we are in prison then we are not free. But there are different sorts of prisons—and it seems that a person can know an inner freedom even in a prison cell. People who seem to be outwardly free can be in a prison inside themselves. Sin is one sort of prison—and fear is another. Jesus came to set us free from the prisons that are within us—and when he told people what he was going to do that was part of the plan:

'The Spirit of the Lord is upon me, because he has chosen me to bring good news to the poor. He has sent me to proclaim liberty to the captives and recovery of sight to the blind; to set free the oppressed and announce that the time has come when the Lord will save his people' (Luke 4:18–19, GNB).

Week 2 / Sunday

Jason Richards

Psalm 51:1-17 (NIV)

I first met Jason in Maidstone Prison. We were in the chapel—with some other prisoners and one of the chaplains—and Jason was playing his guitar as we all sang choruses and songs.

Then all of a sudden he stopped, in the middle of the song. He began talking about the woman at the well in Samaria, and what happened when she met Jesus. It was a meeting that changed her life and transformed her. Jason knew what he was talking about because in Parkhurst Prison he had met Jesus.

I wanted him to tell me about it for this book. Because what happened to that Samaritan woman and to Jason really is good news for a bad and beautiful world.

Jason was in prison for life for murder. When he was 20 he and his brother had committed an armed robbery and killed an innocent bystander. He can never undo what he has done. But he believes that he has been forgiven for it.

Another prisoner had talked to me that same night. Like Jason, he was in for life—for murder. He had become a Christian as well, and it had changed his life on the inside. 'It doesn't matter being in here,' he said to me, pointing at the prison walls, 'because Jesus is in here'—and he thumped his chest.

Perhaps some readers will disapprove of a man who is a murderer having a place in this book. But there are murderers in the Bible. Moses killed a man and had to flee the country. David committed adultery with Bathsheba and then sent her husband into the thick of the battle so that he got killed. Saul who became Paul stood by looking after a pile of cloaks while they stoned Stephen to death—which made him 'an accessory after the fact'. Murder is a terrible sin. But God can forgive even that.

Jason found God and found forgiveness through searching and through reading the Bible. But it was really Jesus who found Jason. He told me how it happened.

'I was in Parkhurst Prison. I hadn't been long in my sentence and I was very confused. About myself and about life. I was carrying an awful lot of guilt. And I was looking for answers. I was trying to work out whether life had any meaning any more. Or whether I knew what meaning was.

'I read a lot. I read Aleister Crowley. I read Buddhism. I read Islam. I started reading the Bible. And the more I read the Scriptures the more I became aware of God.

'I didn't believe in God. I was actually an atheist—or at least I thought I was. But I came to believe that God existed. And the more I became aware of God the more I became aware that I was a sinner—and I got more and more desperate.

'I knew I was alienated from God and that I was beyond the pale. I could see things as light and darkness. I could see the bad side of the world. And the light. I could see what was good. And I knew that I was on the wrong side—and I didn't want to be on that side any more.

'I no longer wanted to identify with the corruption and the greed and the selfishness. I wanted to be on God's side. Yet it was as though I couldn't be. That drove me to a point of desperation. I thought at one stage "Well, if I really work hard, and I try and tell other people about God, then maybe at the end of the day he will say to me: You have made an effort, Jason . . . Maybe then he'll accept me at the last moment."

'But even though I was thinking that I didn't believe it in my heart. I was saying to myself, "You're finished. You're beyond the pale. There is no way that you can make up for what you've been and what you've done. It's impossible."

'Deep down there was this conflict. I could see—like two armies—a darkness and a light. I desperately wanted to change. But I couldn't. Then one night I was in my cell and I just let go totally. My sanity completely went and it was as though I was going into a black hole. Everything seemed to come to an end and there was nothing left.

'Then I just cried out. I actually shouted: "God, have mercy on me!" Then I opened the Bible and it opened up at the psalms. At the very first psalm. I started reading, and then I fell on my knees. And I started crying. I have never wept like that. It was like all of my life went before me. I didn't want to see it. I didn't want to look at it. All of the terrible things.

'I just carried on reading—and when I got to Psalms 50 and 51 I realized that God would forgive me. Psalm 51 was King David's psalm that he wrote after he had had Bathsheba, and had Bathsheba's husband Uriah the Hittite killed. I didn't know all that then. But the thing that I knew was "Save me from bloodguilt, O God, the God who saves me, and my tongue will sing of your righteousness."

'That whole psalm has become my life. Because as soon as I became a Christian I started singing and being involved with music. I'm always singing about God and about my experience of God. It's not something I planned. It's just happened over the years.

'But I knew that God could forgive me. And I just said "OK. I don't care what it is. I'm yours. I'll do whatever you want. That's it. You'll have to teach me." I didn't know anything about Jesus or the Bible or the Church. I just knew. I read all the rest of the psalms on my knees—and almost from that point for me they became psalms of praise. It was like I was beginning to worship—and I didn't know what worship was. I don't know what time I went to bed that night. But I woke up and the whole world was light . . .'

Have mercy on me, O God, according to your unfailing love; according to your great compassion blot out my transgressions. Wash away all my iniquity and cleanse me from my sin.

For I know my transgressions, and my sin is always before me. Against you, you only, have I sinned and done what is evil in your sight, so that you are proved right when you speak and justified when you judge. Surely I was sinful at birth, sinful from the time my mother conceived me. Surely you desire truth in the inner parts; you teach me wisdom in the inmost place.

Cleanse me with hyssop, and I shall be clean; wash me and I shall be whiter than snow. Let me hear joy and gladness; let the bones you have crushed rejoice. Hide your face from my sins and blot out all my iniquity.

Create in me a pure heart, O God, and renew a steadfast spirit within me. Do not cast me from your presence or take your Holy Spirit from me. Restore to me the joy of your salvation and grant me a willing spirit, to sustain me.

Then I will teach transgressors your ways, and sinners will turn back to you. Save me from bloodguilt, O God, the God who saves me, and my tongue will sing of your righteousness. O Lord, open my lips, and my mouth will declare your praise. You do not delight in sacrifice, or I would bring it; you do not take pleasure in burnt offerings. The sacrifices of God are a broken spirit; a broken and contrite heart, O God, you will not despise.

Jason Richards

John 4:4–26 (NIV)

Now he had to go through Samaria. So he came to a town in Samaria called Sychar, near the plot of ground Jacob had given to his son Joseph. Jacob's well was there, and Jesus, tired as he was from the journey, sat down by the well. It was about the sixth hour.

When a Samaritan woman came to draw water, Jesus said to her, 'Will you give me a drink?' ... The Samaritan woman said to him, 'You are a Jew and I am a Samaritan woman. How can you ask me for a drink?' (For Jews do not associate with Samaritans.)

Jesus answered her, 'If you knew the gift of God and who it is that asks you for a drink, you would have asked him and he would have given you living water.'

'Sir,' the woman said, 'you have nothing to draw with and the well is deep. Where can you get this living water? Are you greater than our father Jacob, who gave us the well and drank from it himself, as did also his sons and his flocks and herds?'

Jesus answered, 'Everyone who drinks this water will be thirsty again, but whoever drinks the water I give him will never thirst. Indeed, the water I give him will become in him a spring of water welling up to eternal life.'

The woman said to him, 'Sir, give me this water so that I won't get thirsty and have to keep coming here to draw water.' He told her, 'Go, call your husband and come back.' 'I have no husband,' she replied. Jesus said to her, 'You are right when you say you have no husband. The fact is, you have had five husbands, and the man you now have is not your husband. What you have just said is quite true.'

'Sir,' the woman said, 'I can see that you are a prophet. Our fathers worshipped on this mountain, but you Jews claim that the place where we must worship is in Jerusalem.'

Jesus declared, 'Believe me, woman, a time is coming when you will worship the Father neither on this mountain nor in Jerusalem. You Samaritans worship what you do not know; we worship what we do know, for salvation is from the Jews. Yet a time is coming and has now come when the true worshippers will worship the Father in spirit and truth, for they are the kind of worshippers the Father seeks. God is spirit, and his worshippers must worship in spirit and in truth.'

The woman said, 'I know that Messiah' (called Christ) 'is coming. When he comes he will explain everything to us.' Then Jesus declared, 'I who speak to you am he.'

'That woman's life was totally messed up. Her relationships were obviously not very good because she had had five husbands—plus one, so she had problems with people. But Jesus was able to speak right into that situation and reach her.

'I identify with her in that she was an outcast. She was a Samaritan— and the Jews who were pure Jews ostracized the Samaritans because they had intermarried. But Jesus came along and spoke to her and she couldn't understand it. "Why are you talking to me?"

'It's a bit like what happens here sometimes. I have a good relationship with the guys here on the Thanet wing, which is the Rule 43 wing. They're in there for child abuse or whatever and they are outcasts even within this culture. When you think what some of those guys are in for you think, "Oh my God! How could they do that to somebody?" Particularly when it comes to young children. But none of us are immune from sin, are we? Whatever that sin happens to be.

'One of the things that Jesus did with this woman was that he identified with her as a person. He didn't see her as a Samaritan. He didn't see her as an adulterer. He saw her as a person. So he ws able to cut right through all of the mess.

'If we are totally honest, if Jesus was to walk in here right now and say, "OK, Jason, this is your life! . . . the real life, not all the things that we always want to put on show to people," I would want to crawl under the table. And that's true of all of us. But initially he doesn't even confront us with that. The thing for me is that he confronts me with love, and he says, "Jason, I love you!"

'When my life goes a bit wrong now, what does me in is the fact that he still loves me. I don't feel a rebuke from God. What I feel is an arm, an embrace, and a love that says, "Jason, I love you . . ." That is what actually brings me to my knees all the time. And then whatever the problem is he deals with me graciously.

'I think with the woman of Samaria he dealt with her graciously. He gently confronted her with the realities about her life. And she was able to take that. She was able to receive it from him—I think because he first loved her. And he spoke to her and he just asked her for a simple thing: "Give me something to drink"—and she couldn't handle that at all.

'But then he always takes it one stage further. He said, "Now I can do something for you. This is what you need. The living water." Then he got to the issue of the sin and the husbands. That was later on. It wasn't at the beginning.

'Probably our tendency is to begin with sin. To say, "Look, here is this woman. She's had five husbands and she's living with a guy . . ." But it wasn't like that. With Jesus it was different. And the conclusion of the story is that she recognized him for who he was. She was able to say, "Look, I've found him!" And it was to her that Jesus actually identified himself as the Messiah. "I who speak to you am he." That was the first direct revelation that he gave to anybody. To that woman.'

A promise

On the last and greatest day of the Feast, Jesus stood and said in a loud voice, 'If anyone is thirsty, let him come to me and drink. Whoever believes in me, as the Scripture has said, streams of living water will flow from within him.'

John 7:37–38 (NIV)

Professor Sir Norman Anderson

Hebrews 2:10, 17-18 (NIV)

Norman Anderson used to be Professor of Oriental Laws in the University of London and Director of the Institute of Advanced Legal Studies. He was also Chairman of the House of Laity in the General Synod of the Church of England. He is a prolific writer—his books include *Christianity and Comparative Religion*, *Christianity the Witness of History*, and *Islam in the Modern World: A Christian perspective*.

In bringing many sons to glory, it was fitting that God, for whom and through whom everything exists, should make the author [or 'pioneer'] of their salvation perfect through suffering ... For this reason he had to be made like his brothers in every way, in order that he might become a merciful and faithful high priest in service to God, and that he might make atonement for the sins of the people. Because he himself suffered when he was tempted, he is able to help those who are being tempted.

'I suppose that we all wonder, from time to time, "What is the purpose of human life?—with so much that is happy and beautiful but so much that is sad and ugly, and sometimes evil."

'Well, to my mind this verse tells us the answer. The purpose of God—the One for whom and through whom everything exists—is to bring many sons to glory. His plan is to take ordinary men and women like us—some comparatively good and some far from good, some very happy and some far from happy—and bring them to the wonder of being real sons and daughters of God; part of his family, knowing him as our own loving Father.

'This verse tells us that the way God acted to achieve his purpose was through a pioneer, one who was to lead the way. In Jesus of Nazareth God himself came among us as a man among men. He lived a human life. He was tested and tempted, just as we are. Yet he never became alienated from God. Instead, he always talked and walked with "*Abba*", his own Father, with perfect communion and intimacy. But, unlike Jesus, we are alienated from God, and there is a cloud between us. It's a cloud of sin and failure, and the face of God seems far away. Yet somehow, if life is to mean anything real to us, that cloud has got to go.

'But how could it go? There was a price to be paid for this, as for most things in life, and there is no way in which we could pay it. We can't earn forgiveness. We can't rend that veil. We can't blow away that cloud ourselves. So our pioneer, the Lord Jesus Christ, took it all on himself. He suffered, and he died; he forgave even his executioners.

'Now he offers God's forgiveness to all who repent and look to him in faith; so we can have peace with God. We are set free from our alienation from God, and from our estrangement and our sense of "awayness" from him. If we turn from our own way and throw ourselves on the mercy of God in Christ then we have actually received reconciliation, because in our pioneer we have been reconciled to God.

'There was a price to be paid for forgiveness. The Bible calls this price a ransom, and Christ said that he had come "not to be served but to serve, and to give his life a ransom for many".

'I find this an enormous comfort. I am very conscious of the ways in which I have failed in the past and fail in the present, and it makes all the difference in the world to come to God and say I know that in Jesus Christ my sins are not only forgiven but even forgotten. The cloud has been dispersed and the barrier has gone. In Jesus Christ we have actually become the sons and daughters of God, and we are in a family relationship. We are living life in his presence, he can help us when we are tempted, and God is bringing us to glory.'

A prayer

Father, I delight in the fact that you are my Father—and that you are working out in me your wonderful purpose to bring me to glory, along with many sons and many daughters.*

Terry Waite
Psalm 43:3-5 (NRSV)

In 1986 Terry Waite was talking to me about the peace of the world. It was a summer day, and we were in his room in Lambeth Palace with the sound of London's traffic coming in through the open window. Terry spoke about the relationships between people and between nations— and the possibility of a peace which is a relationship of harmony and compassion. The real, biblical peace of *shalom*—about justice and mercy in every area of life: personal, political and international.

Just six months later, on 10 January 1987, Terry Waite was taken hostage. It was in that week that the original edition of *Lent for Busy People* was published. Right at the start of it were the words that Terry had spoken back in the summer. Three days, beginning with Isaiah 61:1:

The Spirit of the Lord God is upon me, because the Lord has anointed me to bring good tidings to the afflicted; he has sent me to bind up the broken hearted, to proclaim liberty to the captives, and the opening of the prison to those who are bound.

But now Terry himself was bound and in prison—although it wasn't until much later that the world knew the details of his terrible ordeal. He has written about it in *Taken on Trust*, and it is a deeply moving acount of his imprisonment.

Now I wanted to know if what he had said to me on that summer afternoon in Lambeth was still what he believed about relationships between people and nations. His answer was a resounding 'Yes!'

'My views haven't changed at all', he told me. 'In fact they have deepened. What I realized then and realize now is that terrorism, violence, kidnapping, hostage taking, bombing and all those other dreadful acts are hardly ever the primary problem. They stem from the fact that for many years people have had to suffer terrible frustrations.

'I don't justify those violent acts. But if we fail to take account of people who feel (and often are) victimized then we shall continually run into problems of this kind.'

On the day that Terry was saying these things to me, two of the oldest enemies in the Middle East were to make peace. Yitzhak Rabin, the Israeli Prime Minister, and Yasser Arafat of the Palestine Liberation Organization set aside their ancient hatred of each other to sign a peace treaty.

'What a remarkable thing it is,' said Terry, 'and how sad that it has taken so long. I don't want to be cynical, but it seems as if the two principal factors which have brought this about are the collapse of the Soviet Union and (strangely enough) the rise of Islamic fundament-alism. And I was incredibly optimistic for the peace process when I saw people like Ashrawi coming to the fore. I thought that whole process needed the hand and the intervention of an intelligent woman, which she is. Absolutely loyal to her origins, and incredibly able. And she has got that intuition which was so much needed.'

I wondered what Terry had needed to endure his five-year imprisonment, and what help the Bible had been to him when he was finally given one. 'Was there a particular Bible passage?' I asked him. 'No,' he answered, 'because one has to take the Bible as a whole. There is always a temptation to look for comfort by taking a text out of context. Or just taking one text. And in situations of extremity that is very unsatisfying.

'The great message of the Bible is that it tells the truth about human nature. And when you are in solitary confinement and in isolation, and tending to be very introspective, there is a limit to how much truth you can take in at one time. Yet if you allow the light of truth to search you it does so, in an extraordinarily penetrating way, and the truth and the light heal you.

'The healing process is a painful one, but somehow the light and truth lead through an experience of pain to one of reconciliation. I know that reconciliation between people has to go far beyond politics. But it also has to be intimately connected and related to our own inner reconciliation. Psalm 43 can show us the way to reconciliation, and to God.'

O send out your light and your truth; let them lead me; let them bring me to your holy hill and to your dwelling. Then I will go to the altar of God, to God my exceeding joy; and I will praise you with the harp, O God, my God.

Why are you cast down, O my soul, and why are you disquieted within me? Hope in God; for I shall again praise him, my help and my God.

Psalm 43:3–5 (NRSV)

'I believe we can look at the holy hill of God as the hill of Calvary. Whatever happens to us we always have to look at the life of Christ and see what he had to suffer. Severe isolation, loneliness, betrayal and crucifixion.

'All of that has to do with reconciliation—because "in Christ God was reconciling the world to himself, not counting their trespasses against them, and entrusting the message of reconciliation to us..." (2 Corinthians 5:19, NRSV).'

I finished by asking Terry how we could pray about the peace of the world and about reconciliation. 'The prayer would be a very simple one,' he said.

'Oh Lord, we pray for courage to allow your light and your truth to shine into our souls so that we may be healed.'

For the next three days we shall look at Terry Waite's original comments on Isaiah 61. Comments made before his terrible years of imprisonment as a hostage—and that he still stands by even after that soul-searching ordeal.

Terry Waite

Isaiah 61:1 (RSV)

The Spirit of the Lord God is upon me, because the Lord has anointed me to bring good tidings to the afflicted; he has sent me to bind up the brokenhearted, to proclaim liberty to the captives, and the opening of the prison to those who are bound...

'When you consider that Isaiah wrote so many years ago, in a situation of tension and difficulty, those are remarkably tender, compassionate, noble words. They reveal sentiments which accord with our highest and best understanding of what it is to be human.

'"The Spirit of the Lord God is upon me... to bind up the brokenhearted": in other words to have that sensitivity to people and so to enter into their distress that the binding up and healing process is set in motion—in people who don't understand themselves, who have broken relationships with those whom they love, or who are bereaved.

'Healing is to do with relationships, and a healed person is one who is truly whole. So healing is about growing into a whole relationship with yourself, with God and with your neighbour.

'"The Spirit of the Lord God is upon me... to proclaim liberty to the captives..." No one can really claim liberty for others unless they begin to experience it in their interior lives. It isn't just the unlocking of someone from captivity. It is experiencing an inner liberty of spirit, and then being able to share it with others and to proclaim to others the glorious liberty and freedom that comes from being increasingly free within.

'We are composite within—an inherited mixture of light and darkness—and when we try to understand our own complexity we can fall into awful traps. We can say: "I must be walking in the light all the time and suppressing the dark," and then the dark rumbles around and suddenly shoots up and surprises us.

'This is where the Christian understanding of original sin is so important. It shows us our humanity, and because it is such a realistic assessment we are not driven into the opposites of having either a false pride or a false despair. We can have a quiet confidence and a healthy recognition of our own human nature. We can understand our own failings and be reasonably tolerant about them (and that doesn't mean we condone them) and then we have a compassion for the failings of other people, who are just like us, and we can proclaim liberty for them.

'I see "the opening of the prison to those who are bound" in the same way. In a sense we are all bound, by our upbringing and by our culture, and we have to allow our eyes to be opened, so that we can experience more of the true liberty of being, which is something you cannot manufacture. But when it's there people recognize it in your presence—not by what you say, but by who you are and what you are.'

A prayer

Lord Christ, bind up my broken heart; set me free from my captivity; open my prison—then anoint me with your Spirit to bring good tidings to those who are afflicted as I am.*

Terry Waite

Isaiah 61:2-3 (RSV)

The Spirit of the Lord God is upon me ... to proclaim the year of the Lord's favour, and the day of vengeance of our God; to comfort all who mourn; to grant to those who mourn in Zion—to give them a garland instead of ashes, the oil of gladness instead of mourning, the mantle of praise instead of a faint spirit; that they may be called oaks of righteousness, the planting of the Lord, that he may be glorified.

'The "year of the Lord's favour" is the year of Jubilee, the time when people and things were released and set free. I see it as relating to the kingdom of God. We pray "Thy kingdom come", and that kingdom is not of this world. Its essence lies in human and divine relationships. So often in our secular understanding of what it means to build a kingdom, we violate human relationships.

'We engage in violence and in acts that go against the wellbeing of individuals, because we say, "They're nothing more than pawns—so for the sake of a greater cause they can be sacrificed." But once you lose sight of the unique and precious nature of the individual you lose sight of the kingdom, because "the kingdom of God is within you", and that means within individuals. I believe that our relationships with God and with one another lie right at the heart of the kingdom.

' "The Spirit of the Lord God is upon me ... to comfort all who mourn ..." We all mourn, and we have to be able not only to comfort all who mourn but to be comforted ourselves. I was talking once with Chris Bonnington, the mountaineer, about our reactions when people close to us have died. It was on a television interview, and he spoke about the time when he lost his colleagues on the mountain, and of how he lost his own son in an accident. It was years later, but the tears came into his eyes. When you know how bitter an experience it is to lose the physical presence of someone you love you know that the comforting of those who mourn isn't saying, "Well, never mind, it'll be all right."

'Sometimes it's just being quiet with somebody, and allowing their grief to penetrate your own soul. You don't have to say anything. One of the things that comforts me when I'm sad is the knowledge that there are other human beings who know me from all sides. They know the light and the darkness in me, and because of the closeness of the relationship they have experienced not only the light but the unpleasantness of the dark as well. But the relationship proves to be totally and absolutely dependable, and I know that I am still loved and valued and respected as a person, almost in spite of myself.

'It goes back to the kingdom again, which is not all about jubilation and hand-clapping. It's also about the profound depth of human experience with all its emotions.'

A prayer

Lord Christ, give me some of your Spirit to comfort the places in my heart where I hurt ... Then give me some more of your Spirit, so that I can comfort other people.*

Terry Waite

Isaiah 61:4-6 (RSV)

They shall build up the ancient ruins... they shall repair the ruined cities, the devastations of many generations. Aliens shall stand and feed your flocks, foreigners shall be your ploughmen and vinedressers; but you shall be called the priests of the Lord, men shall speak of you as the ministers of our God; you shall eat the wealth of the nations, and in their riches you shall glory.

'This is speaking yet again about the harmony between people. It is implying a most remarkable relationship between people for strangers to come and feed your flocks. This was written in a country where there were wandering tribes, and in order to survive they had to protect their own interests. It is a curious thing for a stranger to come and feed your flock rather than to steal it. That speaks of the kingdom which has to do with relationships between ourselves and God, ourselves and our neighbour, and between nation and nation.

'Isaiah is pointing to a relationship of harmony and compassion that is so often lacking in our mechanical understanding of international affairs, where we seem totally to fail to apply the principles which we say are moral. We say that in order to achieve a certain political end some innocent people will be killed, and it's regrettable but it always happens.

'Yet why should it always happen? Why should the innocent always suffer? Why shouldn't we have higher standards of international morality? If we were to practise the same morality in our interpersonal relationships as we practise in international relationships we wouldn't dare to step outside our own front door.

'So what about having a clearer and deeper examination of the whole area of international morality, and nations being big and generous enough to feed the flocks of others? So that nation really does "speak peace unto nation" ...

A prayer

Lord Christ, show me what I can do for the peace of the world.*

Material for reflection and groups

Ask each person if they are willing to share with everyone something about an area in their own life where they feel they are in prison, or where they once were and are now set free.

Talk about any insights, discoveries or problems that people have as a result of the week's readings.

Finish by using Terry Waite's prayer, followed by 4 or 5 minutes' silence. Then slowly read out Psalm 51 from the end of Sunday.

GOOD NEWS ABOUT THE CREATOR AND THE CREATION

W hen I was in my teens I became an atheist because I thought that science had disproved the existence of God—and there are a lot of people who still think that. But they are wrong. Many scientists believe in God, and many scientists are Christians. This week you will read what three of them have to say about the astonishing wonder of the creation (and about the Creator). John Habgood, the Archbishop of York, is a scientist as well as a theologian, and in the 1950s he was a Demonstrator in Pharmacology at Cambridge. One of his books is *Religion and Science*. Dr David Ingram is the Vice Chancellor of the University of Kent, and used to be a Professor of Physics, and one of his books is *Radiation & Quantum Physics*.

The Revd John Polkinghorne is the only priest in the Church of England who is also a Fellow of the Royal Society. President of Queens' College, Cambridge, he was Professor of Mathematical Physics from 1968–79. His books include *The Way The World Is*, *The Quantum World*, *One World*, *Science and Creation* and *Science and Providence*. Susan Howatch (you will read her in Holy Week) read three of his books in 1990 and found them fascinating.

'This is a very, very exciting thing,' she thought, 'because now religion and science aren't seen as opposed to each other but complementary.' She wanted to set up something in the field of religious education, so she has endowed a lectureship in Cambridge in natural science and theology. All because in 1990 she read John Polkinghorne—and he helped her to set up the lectureship.

Hugh Montefiore, who was the Bishop of Birmingham, is a theologian who is intrigued with the way the world is, and one of his books is *The Probability of God*. He edited *Man And Nature* and has a deep concern for the environment.

Gavin Reid is the Bishop of Maidstone. He used to work for the Church Pastoral Aid Society as their Secretary for Evangelism, and from 1982–85 he was the National Director of Mission England. His books include *A New Happiness, To Be Confirmed, To Reach A Nation* and (jointly written with me) *Lights That Shine* and *Brushing Up On Believing* We are currently writing *Confirmed For Life* which should be published in 1994.

The Revd Dr John Polkinghorne

Job 38:1–18 (RSV)

Then the Lord answered Job out of the whirlwind: 'Who is this that darkens counsel by words without knowledge? Gird up your loins like a man, I will question you, and you shall declare to me. Where were you when I laid the foundations of the earth? Tell me, if you have understanding. Who determined its measurements—surely you know! Or who stretched the line upon it? On what were its bases sunk, or who laid its cornerstone, when the morning stars sang together, and all the sons of God shouted for joy?

'Or who shut in the sea with doors, when it burst forth from the womb; when I made clouds its garment, and thick darkness its swaddling band, and prescribed bounds for it, and set bars and doors, and said, "Thus far shall you come, and no farther, and here shall your proud waves be stayed"? Have you commanded the morning since your days began, and caused the dawn to know its place, that it might take hold of the skirts of the earth, and the wicked be shaken out of it? It is changed like clay under the seal, and it is dyed like a garment. From the wicked their light is withheld, and their uplifted arm is broken. Have you entered into the springs of the sea, or walked in the recesses of the deep? Have the gates of death been revealed to you, or have you seen the gates of deep darkness? Have you comprehended the expanse of the earth? Declare, if you know all this.

'I have always been fascinated by the Book of Job, and by the problem of suffering, which is what the book is about. Job is wrestling all the time with the terrible things that have happened to him. He says that what he really wants is to come face to face with God, because he is certain that God will understand him and not browbeat him. Yet when God does speak to Job out of the whirlwind he speaks in such a strange way.

'First, it's such an inconsequential reply. Job's experience has been so deeply personal, but what God does is to point him to the vast, impersonal world of the universe. Second, it does seem a bit like browbeating, because God says: "I've made this great big world—and who are you? You don't know how it all fits together, Job, or how it works. Have you entered into the springs of the sea or walked in the recesses of the deep?" ... and so on. Nevertheless, I think that strange answer to Job has something very important to say to us, to remind us that although God is concerned with humankind and the existential questions of what is going on inside us, he also has other concerns and other purposes at work in the world. So we have to see ourselves as part of the whole great process of creation.

'As a scientist I'm enormously impressed with the grandeur and order of the world and with the intricate balance of the universe. The world is doing two things at the same time. It is flying apart and expanding because the initial, fiery singularity of the big bang blew it apart, but also gravity is at work pulling it together. If the force of expansion were too strong then the world would fly apart too quickly. It would be too dilute, and nothing would happen. But if contraction were too strong then the world would collapse—it would just fall in upon itself again and get lost in a sort of cosmic melting pot. So you need this very delicate balance between the two, and the accuracy of getting it right has been calculated as equivalent to the accuracy of hitting a target an inch wide at the other side of the universe—which is quite a crack shot! That balance is essential in the processes of the world if they are able to evolve after 15,000 million years such complex and interesting systems as ourselves.

'I'm also interested in the fact that we can understand the world and that it is open to our investigation. To some extent we have "entered into the springs of the sea and walked in the recesses of the deep", because we understand about the structure of matter. Of course there are lots of things that we don't understand, but progressively we are able to do so. The order and balance of the world do seem to me (as they do to many scientists, including those who don't have conventional religious opinions) to speak of there being more to the world than meets the eye. And if we are to search for the deepest possible understanding (which is what scientists are really trying to do), science itself won't be enough—because the given fact of the world is so remarkable, and science simply has to take that for granted. Therefore it has to look outside itself to find a deeper explanation, and for me that lies in the reasons and the purposes of the Creator.

'I think that is what Job is being pointed to here, in terms of the understanding of his day. It is a corrective to a very insistent temptation to think simply in human terms, or simply even in interiorized terms about the life within. Of course if religion doesn't speak about that it is ineffective, but that isn't the only thing it needs to say. Natural theology (which is what comes from looking at the world and seeking the deepest explanation of it) is a corrective to a too greatly man-centred theology, which so often in the end simply turns into anthropology— an account of man rather than an account of God. So that's really why I've chosen this passage, for what it says about the grandeur of the world and the challenge of the world, and about the profundity of the mind that lies behind the structure of the world. It is a reminder that God has other purposes at work in the world, and those purposes are not centred solely upon us.'

Praying

Be still and listen, and allow God to speak to you through some aspect of the world that he has made.

The Revd Dr John Polkinghorne
Job 40:6-7, 15-19; 42:1-6 (NIV)

Then the Lord spoke to Job out of the storm: 'Brace yourself like a man; I will question you, and you shall answer me ... Look at the behemoth, which I made along with you and which feeds on grass like an ox. What strength he has in his loins, what power in the muscles of his belly! His tail sways like a cedar; the sinews of his thighs are close-knit. His bones are tubes of bronze, his limbs like rods of iron. He ranks first among the works of God, yet his Maker can approach him with his sword ...'

Then Job replied to the Lord: 'I know that you can do all things; no plan of yours can be thwarted. You asked, "Who is this that obscures my counsel without knowledge?" Surely I spoke of things I did not understand, things too wonderful for me to know. You said, "Listen now, and I will speak; I will question you, and you shall answer me." My ears had heard of you but now my eyes have seen you. Therefore I despise myself and repent in dust and ashes.'

'What God says here to Job is that "There's more to me than you've got hold of at the moment, and I'm concerned about creatures like behemoth as well as you"—and that leaves Job speechless. Speechless, but not dissatisfied at the end, and that is what is so interesting. Job doesn't get an answer, but God himself is a sufficient answer. We shall never know all the answers—even though we shall never stop asking questions—and when I said that there is a sense in which we have "entered into the springs of the sea" I meant that the world is less mysterious to us now than it was in the days when Job was written. We can see the process of the world more clearly. But as we look at deeper and deeper levels of the world, and (in terms of the subject I used to work in, concerned with the structure of matter) smaller and smaller constituents of the world, so we continually encounter the unexpected, and the world is continually a challenge to us. We never have it all taped, and we always know that if we look round the next corner, or if we explore some regime that we haven't explored before, the chances are that we shall find something we didn't expect and which perhaps we could never even have imagined.

'There is an inexhaustible quality about the world. We don't have it at our command, but we do have a tightening grasp of its reality. We have a better and better understanding of how things work together, and as we gain that understanding we have that absolutely characteristic scientific experience—an experience of wonder and marvel at the very beautiful way the laws of physics work and the balances and structures within them. In fact that's the pay-off for doing science. It's what makes science worthwhile. There is a lot of weary labour in it, and if people didn't get that sort of response they wouldn't do it. Ultimately I think that response of wonder is a religious response—and it's a response which finds no lodging in the world in terms of a scientist's description of it. The impersonal description of science doesn't take into account that experience which is actually one of the fundamental experiences of a scientist. So this is one of the things that points to the incompleteness of science alone—and is the reason why I say we can never have a complete grasp of the world. There is a mystery in human experience which science doesn't have cut and dried and which I don't think we shall ever have cut and dried.'

Praying

Wait on God in silence and allow something to happen. Perhaps when it does happen it will speak to you in a very unexpected way, and for you as for Job it will be a strange answer.

Archbishop John Habgood

Isaiah 40:1–11 (NIV)

Comfort, comfort my people, says your God. Speak tenderly to Jerusalem, and proclaim to her that her hard service has been completed, that her sin has been paid for, that she has received from the Lord's hand double for all her sins.

A voice of one calling: 'In the desert prepare the way for the Lord; make straight in the wilderness a highway for our God. Every valley shall be raised up, every mountain and hill made low; the rough ground shall become level, the rugged places a plain. And the glory of the Lord will be revealed, and all mankind together will see it. For the mouth of the Lord has spoken.'

A voice says, 'Cry out.' And I said, 'What shall I cry?'

'All men are like grass, and all their glory is like the flowers of the field. The grass withers and the flowers fall, because the breath of the Lord blows on them. Surely the people are grass. The grass withers and the flowers fall, but the word of our God stands for ever.'

You who bring good tidings to Zion, go up on a high mountain. You who bring good tidings to Jerusalem, lift up your voice with a shout, lift it up, do not be afraid; say to the towns of Judah, 'Here is your God!' See, the Sovereign Lord comes with power, and his arm rules for him. See, his reward is with him, and his recompense accompanies him. He tends his flock like a shepherd: He gathers the lambs in his arms and carries them close to his heart; he gently leads those that have young.

'This chapter of Isaiah seems to me to have everything. It is one of the great transitional chapters in the Bible. The Israelites in a hopeless situation in exile are given the promise of salvation, and it is on the basis of this kind of vision and prophecy that the movement back to Jerusalem takes place.

'There are many echoes of this chapter in the New Testament, because the theme is resurrection—the resurrection of a people. It has tremendous echoes in our whole culture, in our literature and in our music: you can't read this chapter without mentally singing Handel's *Messiah*. So here is the background against which the New Testament speaks to us. And where the prophecy in verses 3–5 after the proclamation of forgiveness is taken up and subsequently applied to John the Baptist, we have the whole sequence of preparation for the coming of the Lord.

'Then there is the marvellous contrast between the majesty of God and the frailty of human beings. "All flesh is as grass and all their glory as the flower of the field," and this transience is something that we have to come to terms with. Yet in the midst of the transience there is an eternal word of God, and the incomparable God himself, to whom nothing can be compared.

'One of the reasons why I love this chapter is a thought which has haunted me all my life. It was summed up in the title of that book by J.B. Phillips: *Your God is Too Small*. I do not think we can come to terms with the whole glory and beauty and majesty of the world unless our vision of God is greater and more comprehensive—and this is the chapter which gives us that vision.

'I suppose that my scientific background feeds into this vision of God, too, because this is one of the things that every scientist has to do: try to come to terms with the world as it is, in its marvellous complexity and the intricacy of its workings. There is no way of surviving as a scientific Christian without this vision of the majesty of God. And here in this chapter it is set alongside the tenderness of God.

' "The sovereign Lord comes with power—his reward is with him and his recompense accompanies him." But alongside this is the picture of a shepherd with his flock carrying the lambs, and it is this contrast—between the majesty of God and his mercy, and his concern over the very hairs of our head which are all numbered, and also with the stars above—which comes over so superbly.'

A meditation

Sit quietly, and think of a night sky filled with stars.

Then think of a shepherd, carrying in his arms a small, tired lamb who couldn't manage to keep up with the rest of the flock.*

Archbishop John Habgood

Isaiah 40:12–20 (NIV)

Who has measured the waters in the hollow of his hand, or with the breadth of his hand marked off the heavens? Who has held the dust of the earth in a basket, or weighed the mountains on the scales and the hills in a balance? Who has understood the mind of the Lord, or instructed him as his counsellor? Whom did the Lord consult to enlighten him, and who taught him the right way? Who was it that taught him knowledge or showed him the path of understanding?

Surely the nations are like a drop in a bucket; they are regarded as dust on the scales; he weighs the islands as though they were fine dust. Lebanon is not sufficient for altar fires, nor its animals enough for burnt offerings. Before him all the nations are as nothing; they are regarded by him as worthless and less than nothing.

To whom, then, will you compare God? What image will you compare him to? As for an idol, a craftsman casts it, and a goldsmith overlays it with gold and fashions silver chains for it. A man too poor to present such an offering selects wood that will not rot. He looks for a skilled craftsman to set up an idol that will not topple.

'Isaiah has given us a description of the God who measures the waters in the palm of his hand and who is beyond our understanding. God is Lord of the nations, and if the whole earth was given to him as a sacrifice it would not be sufficient as an offering to his glory. Then we come to the crucial question. How do we know God, and how can we describe God?

'This is one of the great mocking denunciations in the Old Testament of the ultimate absurdity of idolatry, and it is still relevant. Human beings are always tempted to make God in their own image or in some form which they can control. So we come back again to the theme, that it is God who is in control of the whole earth. At the end of the chapter we come to the questions which always arise in any discussion of the nature of God. "Well, if God is like this, why doesn't he do more for me? And why is there so much evil and suffering in the world?" The answer comes in those beautiful, familiar words (at the end of the chapter) about the strength which God gives to those who hope in him and wait for him.'

A way to pray

The form of prayer suggested at the end of this chapter, to 'wait' on the Lord, is one of the best things that we can do when we are weary. People sometimes think of prayer as a matter of ferocious activity and concentration. But some of the deepest prayer consists in sitting silently before God, open to him, and simply letting ourself be put into the hands of God, weariness and all.

Notice that this advice to wait comes after this magnificent vision of God, and perhaps a quotation from Baron von Hugel sums it up. He said, 'Think glorious thoughts of God and serve him with a quiet mind.' And this is exactly what this chapter is telling us to do.

It began by speaking about comfort, and that word is made up of two parts: '*com*', which means with, and '*fort*' which means strength. So comfort means that there is a strength with us which is greater than our own strength. And God's people are comforted by knowing that he has not deserted them, even in exile, but that he is with them in his power and that he is going to lead them out of exile into restoration.

It is interesting that in this chapter God is described mostly in negative terms. 'To whom will you compare me, and to what?' The question cannot be answered. 'But lift up your eyes and look at the heavens: who created all these?' The contemplation of the wonder and mystery of the universe, and above all the contemplation of Christ, will send our thoughts in a direction which leads ultimately to mystery and silence, because we are talking about the reality in which everything else consists and without which there would be nothing. It is that reality which is deep in our own selves. It is known in the very fabric of the universe and is the source of unity within it. It is that reality which is the source of its own being. We cannot describe it—which is why in the end Christian description and theology always reach their fulfilment in prayer.

Bishop Hugh Montefiore

Isaiah 40:21-31 (NIV)

Do you not know? Have you not heard? Has it not been told you from the beginning? Have you not understood since the earth was founded? He sits enthroned above the circle of the earth, and its people are like grasshoppers. He stretches out the heavens like a canopy, and spreads them out like a tent to live in. He brings princes to naught and reduces the rulers of this world to nothing. No sooner are they planted, no sooner are they sown, no sooner do they take root in the ground, than he blows on them and they wither, and a whirlwind sweeps them away like chaff.

'To whom will you compare me? Or who is my equal?' says the Holy One. Lift your eyes and look to the heavens: Who created all these? He who brings out the starry host one by one, and calls them each by name. Because of his great power and mighty strength, not one of them is missing.

Why do you say, O Jacob, and complain, O Israel, 'My way is hidden from the Lord; my cause is disregarded by my God'? Do you not know? Have you not heard? The Lord is the everlasting God, the Creator of the ends of the earth. He will not grow tired or weary, and his understanding no-one can fathom. He gives strength to the weary and increases the power of the weak. Even youths grow tired and weary, and young men stumble and fall; but those who hope in the Lord will renew their strength. They will soar on wings like eagles; they will run and not grow weary, they will walk and not be faint.

'I have chosen this chapter because I never read it without my heart being uplifted by the kind of vision of God it gives me. It contains words which were spoken to the Jewish exiles to comfort them—"speak comfortably to my people"—and that gets me in the right mood to listen, because to a certain extent we are all exiles in this world, and we certainly all need to be spoken comfortably to. We are reminded that God loves his people, and cares for them, and we're told that he is the good shepherd.

'But there is nothing cosy about this vision of God. It is a God who loves us and cares for us, but who is infinitely greater than we can begin to imagine or conceive. We know now far more about the works of creation than Isaiah did, but somehow what he says chimes in with our present knowledge of creation. We think of things coming into existence and going out of existence, and this is reflected here. We are told that "all flesh is as grass and grass withers". But in contrast to this there is a transcendence of God over all his creation. "The word of our Lord endures for ever."

'Then there is that amazing comparison between the majesty of God and the contingency of all that he has created. They had a different vision from us of how the world was created, but the picture still holds. "He has measured the waters in the hollow of his hand, meted out heaven [that means the stars, of course] with the span of his hand, comprehended the dust of the earth in a measure [an ephah, which contains 44 pints]."

'What a wonderful vision of a transcendent God with his expanding creation! They probably only thought of the moon as a little pinprick of light. We know now that the sun is a middle-aged star and that we're just one of the many planets whirling round it, smaller than a peanut in comparison with the whole majesty of heaven. We know there are a hundred billion stars in the Milky Way, and billions of different nebulae, and this whole creation is expanding and growing in a way we cannot begin really to understand, so that light from one part has never reached another part of it.

'Yet despite the hugeness of this vast creation God is wholly transcendent over it. He has "weighed" things in his hand. He sits upon the circle of the earth, the inhabitants are like grasshoppers. He stretches out the heavens as a curtain. I love that—"as a curtain" stretching them. That's just what's happening. There's an expanding universe, and he spreads it out as a tent to dwell in.

'So this fills me with a vision of a God who is greater than we can conceive and larger than we can understand. "Who has known the mind of the Lord, the seat of his understanding?"—the understanding that has thought up this mighty cosmos of which we are such an infinitesimal part. Yet at the same time he acts to each one of us as a shepherd. He isn't a God afar off who can be worshipped and adored but before whom we feel totally insignificant and useless. Quite the contrary is true, and the whole passage ends with an affirmation that in him we can find personal renewal.

'We are told that "he gives power to them that faint and to them that have no might he increases strength"—as though to be seized with a vision of this God, to know that though he's so vast yet he cares for each one of us, is to be touched with his renewing power. Because without that power "even the youths shall faint and be weary and the young men shall utterly faint. But they that wait upon the Lord shall renew their strength." It's the combination of thought and poetry which always moves me.

' "They shall mount up with wings as eagles; they shall run, and not be weary; and they shall walk, and not faint." For those of us who look around the state of the world today, and who think of the vastness of the universe compared with our comparative insignificance, it is indeed to be spoken comfortably to to be reminded that we shall "walk and not faint".'

A way to pray

I think this passage is best used not directly in prayer but as a preparation for being able to speak to God as one who is far greater than the world, and yet at the same time cares for us and will listen to us now when we speak to him the secrets of our hearts. So I would like to suggest that it would be helpful simply to read the passage, and then to think about the greatness of God, and to remember that he renews us and cares for us.

Week 3 / Friday

Dr David Ingram

Ephesians 1:4 (NRSV); Revelation 21:1–5 (AV)

'Two particular Scriptures that have always appealed to me both deal with the idea of purpose in God's plans for us. The first is just a single verse . . .'

[God] chose us in Christ before the foundation of the world to be holy and blameless before him in love.

Ephesians 1:4 (NRSV)

'What I like about this rather profound verse is that it makes it clear that Christianity involves a plan which was conceived before space and time came into existence. The plan was there before the foundation of the world, on a grand and exciting scale—not just something that came in as an afterthought. The whole idea of such a verse and concept looks on to the culmination of God's purpose, as does the other Scripture I always link with it—the passage at the end of the Book of Revelation, where John says that he saw a vision.'

And I saw a new heaven and a new earth: for the first heaven and the first earth were passed away; and there was no more sea. And I John saw the holy city, new Jerusalem, coming down from God out of heaven, prepared as a bride adorned for her husband. And I heard a great voice out of heaven saying, Behold, the tabernacle of God is with men, and he will dwell with them, and they shall be his people, and God himself shall be with them, and be their God. And God shall wipe away all tears from their eyes; and there shall be no more death, neither sorrow, nor crying, neither shall there be any more pain: for the former things are passed away. And he that sat upon the throne said, Behold, I make all things new. And he said unto me, Write: for these words are true and faithful.

Revelation 21:1–5 (AV)

'I believe these passages bring a deep sense of purpose into our Christian faith. We spend a lot of our time dealing with ordinary day-to-day affairs and with difficult challenges. It somehow puts those things into perspective to see that Christianity is also concerned with the much longer term. God conceived a plan before space and time came into existence that there should be human beings, who would be given the power to know him and to enter into a relationship with him (that first verse speaks of being "before him in love"), and that plan works right through to an entirely new situation. I think life in this present framework can be likened to a play taking place on a stage.

'Here we are on this planet earth, with wonderful lighting effects and wonderful scenery—but the real point of it all is that the play is on and we, as actors and audience combined, should be trying to discover the message of that play. A play that was written before space and time is going on now and then one day the final curtain will be drawn. Although the play will stop the message of the play worked out in us will carry on into that new creation envisaged in John's vision. That is part of the greatness and grandeur of Christianity, which sometimes we don't appreciate—because we are so immersed in the day-to-day problems on the stage, and have forgotten the name of the author and the meaning of the play itself.

'I think that the point of the play, and the whole of this current existence, is to give us the opportunity to make choices. I believe a soul can be defined as "the sum total of the choices that a person makes", because those choices make the person into what he or she is. I believe that one day this particular space–time continuum in which we live will be taken down and disposed of, because it will have done its job. It will have acted as the stage. But the choices that were made in the play and the people who made them will carry on into that greater reality of the new heavens and the new earth.'

An entry into prayer

In Christianity we are dealing with a mastermind, which had concepts and plans for us long before time began. It is a very great plan and it has magnificent vistas. Nevertheless, part of that plan is that we ourselves, just mere small pieces in the plan, should have an actual relationship with the mind behind it. That is why that verse in Ephesians is so encouraging. It gives us the possibility—and even the right—to approach the One who conceived it all in the first place.

To me that is one of the wonders of Christianity. So a route into prayer is simply to consider the wonder of the plan, and the wonder of the fact that you and I can have a relationship with the God who planned such a part for us and then acted to make it all possible.

Week 3 / Saturday

Bishop Gavin Reid

Romans 8:18–25 (RSV)

I consider that the sufferings of this present time are not worth comparing with the glory that is to be revealed to us. For the creation waits with eager longing for the revealing of the sons of God; for the creation was subjected to futility, not of its own will but by the will of him who subjected it in hope; because the creation itself will be set free from its bondage to decay and obtain the glorious liberty of the children of God. We know that the whole creation has been groaning in travail together until now; and not only the creation, but we ourselves, who have the first fruits of the Spirit, groan inwardly as we wait for adoption as sons, the redemption of our bodies. For in this hope we were saved. Now hope that is seen is not hope. For who hopes for what he sees? But if we hope for what we do not see, we wait for it with patience.

'What I find in this passage is reality. Paul had an absolutely realistic faith that expected sufferings. He didn't think his faith was going to be a way out of suffering: it was a way of coping *with* suffering. In our day a lot of people have what I would call a candy-floss spirituality. Their faith doesn't square with reality, and at the first knock that hits them they feel that God has somehow let them down. Or they think they must have been in the wrong with God for it to happen, but they can't see within themselves what they have done to deserve their illness or adversity, so they are in big trouble.

'But Paul, who made no bones about being justified (being a righteous person because of what Jesus had done, a person who stood tall in God's sight) still says, in spite of all that, that suffering is the lot of the human being. He says that one day creation will be liberated from its "bondage to decay", and he says that "we ourselves who have the first fruits of the Spirit, groan inwardly as we wait for our adoption as sons, the redemption of our bodies".

'It hasn't happened yet. We ourselves are still part of this condition of "bondage to decay". We have to wait patiently for the time when God will wipe away all tears from our eyes.

'One day I was speaking at a conference and I hadn't heard the previous talk, which had been given by a well-known person who saw things differently. I came in all innocence to give the last of a series of talks and had long decided to speak on Romans 8.

' "Let's be quite clear about this," I said, "we are dying people, and we shall all die whatever view of healing we may or may not have. It won't override the fact that we are in bondage to decay, and we must die . . ."

'It is almost laughable, but people were queuing up to thank me for the talk, and saying, "Thank you for giving me the freedom to allow myself to be a dying human being."

'We must allow ourselves to be creatures who grow old and wear out. We may not particularly like it but at least let's not have a spiritual crisis about it. Those people at that conference found release from a whole set of problems simply by realizing that this is part of reality.

'Whatever view of healing we have it must be subservient to the fact that the general condition of the human race is part of the whole condition of the created order. That is, that we live our lives "in bondage to decay". That is our lot this side of glory and we must come to terms with it.

'But being in bondage to decay isn't the last word for humanity. Paul led into all this by saying that "the sufferings of this present time are not worth comparing with the glory that is to be revealed to us", and further on he says, "if we hope for what we do not have, we wait for it patiently". So there is a "now" and a "not yet", and that's a strong New Testament theme. "Now we see through a glass, darkly—but then face to face."

'I find Paul's spirituality a far greater help to me than the slick spiritualities that are on sale today. Therefore suffering doesn't surprise me, and it doesn't surprise me to see through a glass darkly. I don't start saying, "What have I done wrong, God, that I can't see more clearly?" It's the will of God that this is the way it is at the moment. But one day it will be different.'

A reflection

Reflect for a few moments on the way the world is—'in bondage to decay'. Then reflect on the words that 'the sufferings of this present time are not worth comparing with the glory that is to be revealed to us.'*

Material for reflection and groups

Ask people to say if they think that science disproves the existence of God.

Talk about the way you perceive the creation and the Creator—and say whether this week's readings have enlarged your view.

Finish by reading out Isaiah 40:21–31 at the start of Thursday, and then reflect on it in the way that Bishop Hugh Montefiore suggests at the end of the day. Then read the passages at the beginning of Friday, and read out Dr David Ingram's suggestion for 'An entry into prayer'. Be silent for 4 or 5 minutes, and end with the Lord's Prayer.

GOOD NEWS ABOUT THE GOD WHO SPEAKS TO US

That marvellous letter to the Hebrews begins by saying that 'In the past God spoke to our forefathers through the prophets at many times and in various ways, but in these last days he has spoken to us by his Son, whom he appointed heir of all things, and through whom he made the universe. The Son is the radiance of God's glory and the exact representation of his being, sustaining all things by his powerful word' (Hebrews 1:1–3).

The good news is that God has spoken to us—and he hasn't stopped speaking. He continues to speak to us through the words of the Old Testament and the New—and several of the people who have contributed to this week tell how he has spoken to them in the past and how he still speaks.

Christians believe that God created us to have a love relationship with him. A relationship that the Bible likens to that of parent and child, and of husband and wife. A spiritual relationship that is far more intimate and total than a human marriage. So it isn't surprising that God does speak to us—because all good relationships are marked by the depth and the quality of their communication.

Week 4 / Sunday

Bishop Gavin Reid

Romans 8:26–28 (RSV)

Likewise the Spirit helps us in our weakness; for we do not know how to pray as we ought, but the Spirit himself intercedes for us with sighs too deep for words. And he who searches the hearts of men knows what is the mind of the Spirit, because the Spirit intercedes for the saints according to the will of God. We know that in everything God works for good with those who love him, who are called according to his purpose.

'This passage continues on from yesterday's, and it's important to see that the well-known verse that we end with today is set in the context of facing up to tribulation and being in bondage.

'Paul is saying that even the things that we see going wrong can be part and parcel of an overall pattern that God is weaving. One day we'll look back and say, "Wasn't it a good pattern?!" God is working his purposes out—but at the time we don't always see it.

'In this talk about God being able to work everything together for good, that "good" must mean our fulfilment and well-being. That doesn't necessarily mean that "I'm firing on all mental, emotional and spiritual cylinders—so 10 out of 10." And it doesn't mean that I finish up at the end of the story having inherited a bigger sum of money than I had before.

'Our true well-being is related to our closeness to God. There is a deep fulfilment in realizing that one is actually playing a part in the working out of God's purposes in the world. Christianity is about doing as well as being. Both matter. Eastern religion overbalances on the "being", but I think we are meant to be people who can look back on our lives and say,"By God's grace I did something useful, and it was worthwhile."

'This passage also says something very interesting about prayer. I think it is saying, "You worry far too much about prayer... prayer is happening all the time. Is God in touch with you?" "Yes." "Then does God know what's in your mind?" "Yes." "Is the Holy Spirit in your life?" "Yes." And if all these things are true, you can't say that God doesn't know what's bugging you and what's elating you and everything in between! The answer has to be "Yes, he does."

'I think prayer starts by stopping—and realizing that you may not be very good at doing things, but God is actually in touch with your spirit. He knows what's going on and what are your longings and your rejoicings. So why don't you, as it were, just listen to what God is hearing from you?

'I'm not for a moment wanting us to stop the practice of prayer, but I have never met a Christian who wouldn't say there are times when they find a barrenness in prayer and a difficulty in practising prayer. I think they have to be reassured that there is still prayer going on. God is not someone who says, "Sorry, I haven't heard from you today so therefore I don't know what you want."

'It is interesting that this passage comes in the context of living a life that involves sufferings, because a lot of our sufferings are things that affect our ability to pray—particularly if we are emotionally hit, and that's just as normal a suffering as if we're physically hit.'

A way to pray

Start with the understanding that, because of the Holy Spirit, prayer is happening anyway. It is of great benefit to become self-conscious of this. Conscious praying is not about starting and stopping a time of communication with God. It is the entering more fully into what is already happening.

I sometimes think that prayer is almost like taking part in a divine committee meeting, in which we are entering into the affairs of the kingdom, which is a far richer concept than merely talking to God about what worries me. I'm making my contribution to the committee meeting, where God as chairman is going to draw up the conclusions having heard all the contributions.

I find this sort of praying means that early in the day I have to tune in to that self-consciousness of what is happening. Some sort of exercise which makes me conscious of being a praying person has got to be done, and this is not particularly to do with whether it takes half an hour or five minutes.

If I can only spend a few minutes in prayer I don't have any guilty feelings, but I would if I hadn't spent any time, because I need to open up the lines of communication and to be aware. Prayer for me from that moment on is simply becoming aware of the praying that's going on—whether I'm in the car or wherever I am—and saying, 'Yes Lord, I am saying this to you.' That is basic prayer and for me everything else is an overlay on that.

Martyn Lewis

Luke 2:29–32 (RSV)

A recent article about Martyn Lewis in the *London Evening Standard* headlined him as 'The cosy revolutionary who's put the cat among the cynics.'

'As a revolutionary leader', wrote Matthew Norman and Nicholas Hellen, 'the chipmunk-featured newsreader cuts an unlikely figure. By most standards, let alone those of our television networks, he is a meek and mild man—a solid Christian, a keen worker for charities, an optimist and, most famously, a lover of household pets both feline and canine.'

What Martyn Lewis has been in revolt about for some time (he only went public a few months ago) is that news values on television are unfairly biased towards the negative.

'The reaction from his own profession was one of withering scorn,' says the article, 'as Jeremy Paxman and Peter Sissons (among many others) "put the boot in" ... flicking away his argument as soppy, sentimental cobblers ... But Lewis just kept chugging away, and the letters of support started arriving, not only from the public but also from the Archbishop of Canterbury and the Prince of Wales.'

He knew it was an unconventional line to take, and he knew it might damage his career. When he spoke to me on the phone it was from the Nine O'clock News office.

I wanted to talk to him for this book because it seemed to me that as a Christian in the media he was doing just what he should be doing (and what we should all be doing, in our own field). Arguing passionately for the truth—because to tell half a story, or only the bad news stories, isn't 'to live according to the truth' (1 John 1:6). It is to look at all the bad bits of the world and not the good ones.

'It's not so much a choice between good news and bad news,' Martyn Lewis said. 'It's not saying, "Let's have more good news and let's have less bad news." What I'm saying is that we ought to be more willing than we are in the news business to acknowledge the good news stories when they happen.

'There is a tendency in some (not all) television news organizations to create programmes that are based on the degree of disaster or conflict they can reflect. And in some regional television terms the choice of stories seem to come largely from the local police station and nothing else.

'What I am talking about is tilting the balance back by no more than 10 or 15 per cent. If you cover a story about a person or an organization or a company or a country when things are going wrong for them, then it seems to me that the very least you should do is go back and report it when things are going right for them.

'You have got to have a news peg in order to do it. That is a very important qualification. But even when the news peg is there we tend still not to run the story. We have got to the stage where we are leaving an impression in viewers' minds of organizations and people and countries which is very negative, when that might not be the latest up-to-date position. 80 per cent of people regard television news as their primary source of information. So we have an ability to shape people's perception in a way that no other television or radio programme has and no other media has.

'Let me give you an example. Four or five months ago the truck manufacturer Leyland Daf went into receivership. It was all over television and the newspapers. After a week or so people lost interest and moved on to other things. But after three months there was a hugely successful management buy-out that saved 700 jobs. But at least two of our national television programmes didn't report that—and because they didn't report it the people who rely on those programmes as their main source of information didn't know the facts.

'If you asked them about Leyland Daf they would say "Oh yes, that's the company up in the North West that has gone into receivership." They wouldn't know that it had been rescued. So if you don't redress the balance in some way when the peg is there then I think cumulatively you can create a very unrepresentative picture of the world.

'What I don't agree with is what some of my colleagues say, that news has got to be that which is bad. The mistake we made in the past is to think that good news means the light, funny story at the end of the programme. What I am saying is that there are serious positive news stories out there about important issues that deserve to be recognized and identified and not put on the spike or pushed to one side. Not demoted from the bulletin—as they often are now.

'I am not suggesting that we do light and trivial stories, which some people have caricatured me as wanting. I simply believe that when we come to assess the editorial priorities of the day we ought to be more prepared than we are to weigh the positive stories on the same set of journalist scales on which we weigh the negative. The criteria ought not to be the extent of conflict or disaster or tragedy. The criteria ought to be the extent to which that story shapes or changes, or has the potential to shape or change, the country or the world in which we live.'

I wondered what he thought about the stories in the Bible. 'The Bible is a quite a good example of my argument,' he said, 'because it does redress the balance. It paints a lurid and sometimes a bloodthirsty picture of things when they're going wrong—but then when things start to go right it tells you that as well. It goes into a lot of detail about what's wrong—but I think we could learn a little from it in explaining about things going right.

'I feel a deep sadness when we see some of the tragedies happening in the world. You wonder why God would allow some of the things to happen that are happening—particularly in Bosnia, where this ethnic cleansing is going on. It pulls you up short in the news room when you see the details of the report coming in.'

'But don't people have to be free if they are going to make choices?' I said to him. 'God can't keep sticking his oar in. If we throw a brick through a window he can't turn it into a balloon, can he? Not if we're to be free?'

'No, that's true,' he said, 'and if we are to be free then some people will be influenced by ungodly thoughts. When you look at countries like Bosnia and Northern Ireland, where people are living so far in the past, it is sometimes unthinkable that some of them are of this world. I just wish that people could free themselves from their past much more easily. Then they would realize that we are all human beings.'

In the week that Martyn Lewis talked to me there was some very good news around—and Israel and Palestine were about to sign a peace treaty. I had asked him to choose a passage from the Bible, and because of current events he picked Luke 2:29–32. 'I just thought it was rather apt,' he said, 'in view of the Middle East peace talks, and the peace agreement which has started—and will hopefully come to fruition over the next few years.'

Lord, now lettest thou thy servant depart in peace,
according to thy word;
for mine eyes have seen thy salvation
which thou hast prepared in the presence of all peoples,
a light for revelation to the Gentiles,
and for glory to thy people Israel.

Think and pray

Think about your own attitude to the news. How does it affect you when you hear bad news? How do you think it is affecting our world—to hear all the bad news and hardly any of the good news? Pray for Christians in the media.

'You will know the truth, and the truth will make you free.'

John 8:32

'The inquiry of truth, which is the love-making or wooing of it, the knowledge of truth, which is the presence of it, and the belief of truth, which is the enjoying of it, is the sovereign good of human nature.'

Francis Bacon, *The Moral and Historical Work of Francis Bacon*

'Behold, thou desirest truth in the inward being; therefore teach me wisdom in my secret heart...'

Psalm 51:6 *

Week 4 / Tuesday

Wendy Craig

Isaiah 55 (NIV)

Wendy Craig is well known to millions of people through television, and 'Butterflies' and 'Nanny' were two of her most popular series. I knew she was a Christian, so I asked her if she would talk to me about her faith and link it to a passage from the Bible.

She said she would, and when we spoke on the phone to fix up the interview I asked her which passage it was going to be. But she said she wasn't sure yet, because God seemed to speak to her through whatever she happened to be reading at the time.

So we both thought it would be a good idea for her to pick one about listening to God—because it really is good news for a bad and beautiful world: that if we listen for it we can hear the voice of God.

When I finally knocked at her front door (I had got lost—and only found the way because I met two girls on horseback who knew where she lived) I heard her familiar voice reassuring me that the door would be open as soon she had undone the locks. She welcomed me in out of the pouring rain, settled me in her sitting room, and went to make us some tea.

As we started talking she told me about an experience she had when she was away from home. 'I was in a hotel room—and because I was so tired I was getting panic attacks. Panicking that I'd never be able to remember my lines, and that I'd never be able to make my lips say the things my brain knew it had to say. I was working myself up into such a state. And I usually take my Bible with me—but I'd forgotten it, and I was desperate. I pulled open the drawer and there was a Gideon Bible. So I opened the psalms and I leafed through them. And I came across one and I can almost quote it. "I called upon the Lord and he heard me, and he made me bold and stouthearted." I said, "Lord, that's exactly what I want to hear! I'm going to be bold and stouthearted." And my fear just went. I went on to the set the next day—and I got through it without any fear, totally confident in the Lord. But do you know that I've never been able to find that psalm since.' (It is in fact Psalm 138:3 in the New International Version—but it wasn't easy to find.)

The passage that she had chosen was Isaiah 55, and she started to read it out:

Come, all you who are thirsty, come to the waters; and you who have no money, come, buy and eat! Come, buy wine and milk without money and without cost. Why spend money on what is not bread, and your labour on what does not satisfy? Listen, listen to me, and eat what is good, and your soul will delight in the richest of fare. Give ear and come to me, hear me, that your soul may live.

'That's wonderful, isn't it?' she said, ' "Your soul will delight in the richest of fare . . . hear me, that your soul may live." I love this whole chapter. When things really speak to me I've started to put them in this book.'

She had a slim notebook on her lap, and she looked through its pages. 'I haven't got very many so far,' she said, 'but I do write them down. All the verses that really speak to me over certain problems or events. And I think I had written down somewhere in this book about Isaiah 55— but I'm not very well organized. Some people have everything on computer and it must save them so much time. But it's such a wonderful chapter . . .' She began to read again:

You will go out in joy and be led forth in peace; the mountains and the hills will burst into song before you, and all the trees of the field will clap their hands.

'Living in the country that really speaks to me—and it's so true. When I go out in the morning and perhaps it's windy, and the trees are waving about and the grass is swaying—and the whole world is praising him. It's so magnificent!'

Seek the Lord while he may be found; call on him while he is near. Let the wicked forsake his way and the evil man his thoughts. Let him return to the Lord, and he will have mercy on him, and to our God, for he will freely pardon. 'For my thoughts are not your thoughts, neither are your ways my ways,' declares the Lord. 'As the heavens are higher than the earth, so are my ways higher than your ways and my thoughts than your thoughts. As the rain and the snow come down from heaven and do not return to it without watering the earth and making it bud and flourish, so that it yields seed for the sower and bread for the eater, so is my word that goes out from my mouth: It will not return to me empty, but will accomplish what I desire and achieve the purpose for which I sent it.'

'I mostly hear his word when I'm reading it,' said Wendy. 'But sometimes, very occasionally, it is almost as if he is speaking and saying "Do this..." Just a quiet word.

'When I first became a Christian I went through a great patch of not knowing what to do and not knowing which way to turn. I always pray when I'm out walking the dog because it's the only time I get any solitude, and I found myself saying, "Oh God, show me! Tell me! Help me!" I was battering away at God and not listening at all.

'I found myself writing a song called *Show me the way*—which came from going along saying, "Show me, show me! Tell me!" After I had written the song I heard in my head God clearly saying, "Why don't you listen? Why don't you stop shouting and listen?" And from that time I haven't shouted at God any more. I realize you don't go round shouting at God. You just ask him respectfully.'

'I shout!' I said. 'Well, so do I sometimes,' she admitted, 'if I'm in a state. But he knows why, I'm sure. I'm not angry with him. I'm angry with myself. But before I was frustrated with him. It is quite an important thing in my life that I have had to learn to listen to God,' Wendy said, 'and it's only that way that I can really draw near and get the answers.'

I wondered what else was in her book, and she turned over the pages to look. 'Here's one', she said. 'Being in show business there is a lot of fear involved. Fear of actually performing. Not exactly stage fright, but a fear of going on. We're always standing behind scenery waiting to go on. And quaking. "The Lord will rescue me from every evil attack and will bring me safe into his heavenly kingdom. To him be the glory." I always think fear is an evil attack. It's an attack from Satan. He really goes for the jugular with fear.

'Here's another lovely one, from one of Paul's letters. "I can do all things through Christ..." If you say that calmly to yourself before you have to do something, and really believe that Christ will uphold you, it's wonderful.

'This is the last one I wrote,' she said. ' "This is what the Lord says: Stand at the crossroads and look; ask for the ancient paths, ask where the good way is, and walk in it, and you will find rest for your souls." That's Jeremiah, and I think it was again helping me with a decision.'

I wanted to know, finally, how Wendy listens to the voice of God and talks to him, and also how someone else might set about doing that if they weren't used to it. She thought for a moment.

'I suppose it's different for everyone. Certainly God speaks to us in the Bible. But I've found that what helps is not just saying prayers at special moments of the day, but actually keeping close to God all through the day if you possibly can. While you're peeling the potatoes or laying the table, or driving or walking. Just keeping close to him and having little mental chats with him.

'I might say "I'm worried about my friend's daughter. My friend is anxious, because she seems to be taking the wrong path and getting involved with the wrong peple. And she fears she may be taking drugs. I wonder if you could help me with this?" And just bringing things like that to him all the time and really treating him as a loving father. You find yourself getting into conversation with him mentally. Though sometimes I talk to him out loud, often I find myself saying, "Thank you, Lord" or, "Praises, Father" because of some special joyous moment he's given me.

'I think the more time you spend with the Father the more he is able to communicate with you. I really have found that from experience. Sometimes, if I don't spend a lot of time with him, when I am deeply involved in work, or I have pushed him away for some reason because I've got other things to think about, I really get withdrawal symptoms.

'I feel he has turned his back on me. But in actual fact he hasn't at all. I've turned mine on him. He is always there for us. I'm sure he is. If ever you speak to him he is there listening. Because he wants us to speak to him and he wants us to be friends with him.

'But so often we just pretend he isn't there, or we don't acknowledge the fact that he's there, and we think we can manage on our own. I think that the more time we spend with him the richer our relationship with him is. And the more likely we are to hear him.'

Bishop Michael Marshall

John 6:66-68 (NRSV)

Because of this many of his disciples turned back and no longer went about with him. So Jesus asked the twelve, 'Do you also wish to go away?' Simon Peter answered him, 'Lord, to whom can we go? You have the words of eternal life.'

'After I had been ordained for three years I had a breakdown. For quite a time I wasn't really much good to anybody, and I pulled out for about four or five months. At the end of that time I went to a private retreat in Nashdom Abbey. I had a cell there, and one day after lunch I fell asleep.

'Then I woke up—and I just opened the Scriptures, literally, at John 6. I know now (in a sense) what happened to Augustine (and I think to many other Christians). Because the words just sprang off the page. Those words of Peter—almost a cry of despair . . . but also a cry of hope. "Lord, to whom can we go? You have the words of eternal life." And I burst into tears.

'Tertullian speaks about the baptism of tears, and I think there is healing in that experience. I was able to cry. And for a long time afterwards, even when I used the name of our Lord in public— "Jesus"—tears would well up.

'Our Lord was present with me in the room. And because of that I would want to speak of the Scriptures for me as a book of presence. Not only a book of authority. That is one side of it. But the other side is a book of presence. Our Lord does make himself known . . . and when the word of God is read in the Spirit of God by the people of God, then the Word of God makes himself known to us. In just the same way as in the sacrament. It's as strong as that.

'So for me that was another way of reading the Scriptures. To see them as a book of presence—and realize that our Lord makes himself present to us through them, by the overshadowing of the Holy Spirit. "He will glorify me," Jesus told the disciples, "because he will take what is mine and declare it to you" (John 16:14, NRSV). "He will represent me to you" is what he was saying—and for me that is what happened. It was a moment of healing and assurance—and a very beautiful moment.'

A way to pray

See a picture of those disciples in your mind's eye—and then put yourself into the picture. Or into the dialogue. Pray Peter's words for yourself: 'Lord, to whom can I go?' That's the way I pray it, when I am tempted to despair and when I am tempted to give up. 'In the end, Lord, to whom can I go but you?'

Lord Tonypandy

John 15:1-5 (AV)

Lord Tonypandy met me in the central lobby of the Houses of Parliament. He was the Speaker of the House of Commons from 1976 to 1984—and some years earlier, when he was George Thomas, the Labour MP for Cardiff West (and I was an MP's secretary) we had both been members of the House of Commons Christian Fellowship. His autobiography, *George Thomas: Mr Speaker* was a bestseller, and he has also written *The Christian Heritage in Politics*. His way with words and his beautiful Welsh oratory still find expression in his speaking and his preaching, and as well as being in great demand as a speaker he is a Methodist lay preacher.

He led me down the winding corridors of the Palace of Westminster into one of the interview rooms in the basement—and opened up his Bible at the passage he had decided to talk to me about...

I am the true vine, and my Father is the husbandman. Every branch in me that beareth not fruit he taketh away: and every branch that beareth fruit, he purgeth it, that it may bring forth more fruit. Now ye are clean through the word which I have spoken unto you. Abide in me, and I in you. As the branch cannot bear fruit of itself, except it abide in the vine; no more can ye, except ye abide in me. I am the vine, ye are the branches: He that abideth in me, and I in him, the same bringeth forth much fruit: for without me ye can do nothing.

'I picked on these verses because the drama has always attracted me. On the last night the crowd gathered round Jesus—and he had enough insight into the ways of the world and of men to know that it was probably the last time he would be with them. So our Lord, who I am sure always weighed his words carefully, would now weigh them particularly carefully, because he would know that afterwards they would go over that conversation time and time again... He was summing up his ministry—that although he wouldn't be there, yet his Spirit would be living in them: "Abide in me, and I in you..."

'The last thought that he leaves them with is that we are never separate from him, and for me that's been a comfort and a strength all my life: in bereavements, in disappointments, and in trouble—or if I've said something and I wish I hadn't.

'I've always found it easy to talk with God. Wherever I've been in my travels—in desert or mountain or city, far across the world—I've never felt anywhere that I wasn't able to talk with God. Mind you, I think I may make it difficult for God to get a word in sometimes!

'When I pray and talk to him I start off with gratitude, but then I ask that I'll be able to guard my tongue—and that I shall be able to show to other people the compassion which I have received myself.

'I would talk to God when I was walking in the Speaker's Procession, from the Speaker's House into the Chamber. I was automatically following step by step with the others—but they didn't know that in my mind and in my heart I was waiting upon God.

'I think the reason why it's the Christian countries that started parliamentary democracy is that it's the Christian faith which has brought a new emphasis on the importance of the individual.

'I believe that wherever there is a human being, God is there, and that there is something of the divine in every baby born. That has helped me in politics, because it leads straight to the importance of the individual. There is nobody who is unimportant anywhere in the world, and that's the reason why Christians are bound to be concerned about the housing conditions, the education opportunities, and the general standard of living. Not only of themselves but of their neighbours.

'I am the son of a miner and we were poor. When I was a little boy there was a great watermill with a wooden wheel outside the big building, and the stream which used to turn the wheel round raging down from the mountainside—so the place was called "the sound of the watermill"—Tonypandy. The word "*ton*" is Welsh for "tune".

'When I went home last weekend to lovely Tonypandy I looked at the ruins of the old mill, and I realized that poor as we'd been we were rich, because we were always occupied with constructive things. The church itself was our speaking class—although we didn't call it a speaking class. We just called it "drama group", and we hardly realized the leadership that we were being given by the minister and the deaconess.

'When I think of the heritage that I have received through growing up in a Christian home then I think again of those words—"Abide in me, and I in you." They speak to you and they burn into your heart. We can never be separated from the love of God—and love is stronger than death.'

A way to pray

I believe the way we can abide in Christ is by remembering that he told us to pray. We aren't like the saints of old, who got up at five o'clock every morning to pray. But whether it's short or long we can have a period of meditation every day. We can pray the prayer he taught us—the Lord's Prayer. And all through the day we can talk to him.

The Revd Bill Sykes

Ephesians 3:14–17 (RSV)

Bill Sykes is Chaplain Fellow of University College, Oxford. As a priest he lost his faith and struggled to find it again in an unusual way. As well as taking a fresh look at the Bible and theology he explored a great range of literature, poetry, art, science, philosophy and music. It didn't take him very long to rediscover his faith—renewed and enlarged— and BRF has published *Visions of Love* and *Visions of Hope*, anthologies of some of the material he has gathered over the years. *Visions of Faith* and *Visions of Glory* will be published in the next two years.

For this reason I bow my knees before the Father, from whom every family in heaven and on earth is named, that according to the riches of his glory he may grant you to be strengthened with might through his Spirit in the inner man, and that Christ may dwell in your hearts through faith…

'I have chosen this passage because I am very keen on "the God within". In the Genesis story of the creation of man, God fashions and shapes man in his own image and likeness—and the last thing he does is to breathe into man, and man becomes a living being.

'I take that to mean all of us have an enormous source of life in the depth of our souls. If we want to see this fully worked out in a life we can go to the person of Jesus Christ. I think he found something of the Father in the depth of himself. And also he discovered there some of the divine attributes—such as life, light, truth, joy and love.

'One of the important things the Apostle Paul discovered was that it is possible for all of us to experience in some measure what Christ had experienced. In one of his letters he wrote, "it is no longer I who live, but Christ who lives in me." (Galatians 2:20). And even more importantly, "in him all the fullness of God was pleased to dwell" (Colossians 1:19) and, "you have come to fullness of life in him" (Colossians 2:10).

'The reason why I have chosen this passage (and the next few verses, which we shall look at tomorrow) is that in it Paul is coming out with some of those truths. For instance, he wrote "that according to the riches of his glory he may grant you to be strengthened with might through his Spirit in the inner man". That is about God dwelling in us—and my understanding of glory is that it is an experience of the presence of God.

'In the Old Testament, glory was the *shekinah* and it was outside. But after Christ's life and death and the coming of the Holy Spirit, the glory which he experienced can actually come alive in the depths of our souls. I think it was through a vision of somebody living with this glory emanating through him that I really came to faith in Christ. So Paul's prayer is that the riches of his glory might be found within us, and also that we be strengthened with power. One of the gifts of the Holy Spirit is that of might and power. But it doesn't just end there. The passage goes on: "and that Christ may dwell in your hearts through faith".

'I used to imagine Christ as being rather anaemic—not an exciting person at all. But over the years I have changed my mind. I now believe he is a full-blooded person—fully God and fully man—and that in himself he discovered the presence of all these attributes. So when we talk about Christ dwelling in our hearts through faith we need to think of not just the person of Christ but also of the Father and the Holy Spirit along with these divine attributes.'

A way to reflect

Go back to this passage and repeat slowly to yourself some of the words that I have just pointed out. 'That according to the riches of his glory...' Pause on the phrase 'riches of his glory'. Whisper it to yourself several times... and think about it and feel about it.

Let your imagination play a part in all this ... and your intuition. And maybe something of those seeds of glory and riches might come alive in you and begin to permeate your being, so that you begin to be transformed by 'the riches of his glory'.

The Revd Bill Sykes

Ephesians 3:17–19 (RSV)

... and that Christ may dwell in your hearts through faith; that you, being rooted and grounded in love, may have power to comprehend with all the saints what is the breadth and length and height and depth, and to know the love of Christ which surpasses knowledge, that you may be filled with all the fullness of God.

'Paul is still developing his theme in the last part of verse 17, praying "that you, being rooted and grounded in love ..." One of the attributes of God is love, indeed his very nature is love. Not a distant love, but something that comes right into the heart of us and takes root in the depths of us. I think this was Paul's experience, something he knew at first hand. He goes on with his prayer: "that you, being rooted and grounded in love, may have power to comprehend with all the saints what is the breadth and length and height and depth ..." He isn't writing about a narrow, blinkered faith here, but about something immense; an enormous resource of life that is right there in the depth of our being.

'Once this comes alive it is as though scales are removed from our eyes—and we see something of "the God out there". We do live in a beautiful and bad world. But when our eyes are opened through experiencing the divine in ourselves we are able to see something of the divine not just within ourselves but throughout creation. We see with new eyes. And this helps us to cope with the bad and the evil in the world.

'And then the prayer continues that with all the saints we should "know the love of Christ which surpasses knowledge". The pursuit of academic knowledge is very important in University College. But here is something greater than academic knowledge. Of course I don't trumpet that around to the dons or the tutors. I accept that they are experts in their field. But I have this secret and glorious feeling that there is something far more important than academic knowledge. The knowledge mentioned in this passage is connected with knowledge but it refers to a personal knowledge—an awareness of the divine in the depth of our being. When the Old Testament talked of 'knowledge' the reference was usually that of sexual intercourse. Adam 'knew' Eve his wife and she conceived. And this fits in with this deep, inner, intimate, personal knowledge.

'Then the final words: "that you may be filled with all the fullness of God". That is absolutely spot on! And it is a radiant ending to this particular passage.

'Now you may say, "That's all very well, but how does all this happen?" And I would want to point to two main ways. One would be baptism. Baptism has a cleansing element but also a large element of rebirth. A new birth. A triggering, a catalysing of something of the divine already in us and bringing into being new life, divine life.

'The words of the service say: "I baptize you in the name of the Father [which is in the nature of the Father, in the personality of the Father], and of the Son, and of the Holy Spirit." That speaks of this enormous resource already within us but which needs to be triggered off to come alive and to permeate our being. So that is the formal way in which it comes alive.

'But I also think there are informal ways of all this coming alive. God has his own secret passages of coming into human lives. Some people will see something of great beauty in nature that will trigger off something of the divine in them. Conversely, they may come across something disasterous that causes their old valuation of things to shatter. But if they work it through, it can lead to a new life and a new evaluation—and a finding of the life of God within. So those are two ways in which this divine life might grow within us.

'But you might go on then to ask, "And how is this life nurtured? Is it purely by going to church... to matins, or evensong, or perhaps communion?" And my answer would be that all these will be a help. Over the years I have come to see the Eucharist in a different way. At one level we receive bread and wine. But at another level we receive the body and blood of Christ. And in the body and blood of Christ there is also the Father present, and also the Spirit—together with life, light, truth, joy and love. So for me the Eucharist has become a very important service—with its element of thanksgiving for the gifts received.

'But I would want to go on to a rather more informal method and I would like to call it reflection. It is what I suggested we might do yesterday with the start of this passage from Ephesians. We shall do the same thing in a moment with the rest of the verses. Saying them out loud, and repeating certain phrases slowly. Letting them sink in, and thinking about them and getting in touch with one's feelings about them. It is a real way of transformation. So I am very keen on the use of silent reflection as a way of growing—so that a passage from the Bible can come alive in a new way.

'Another thing that people have found helpful is to have a clipboard and pen and paper, and as they reflect over "the riches of his glory"— or whatever passage they are looking at—they might come across something to write down which might be very valuable to them. And the important thing is that they have discovered it for themselves—a truth that they have experienced. Also, I know that people have found the two anthologies useful for reflecting and growing in this way.'

A reflection

Read the rest of the passage slowly. Either out loud or silently. Stay with one or two of the phrases—and think about them and feel about them. If something particular comes to you, then write it down—and remember it.

Material for reflection and groups

[A NOTE: For this week's final meditation everyone will need a notebook or a clipboard and a pen.]

Ask people to say how they believe God speaks to them (if they do believe it).

Talk about the way that God has spoken to the contributors in this week, and about anything new you have discovered from what they say.

Use the 'Think and pray' section at the end of Martyn Lewis' piece. Then read out Bill Sykes' method of reflection at the end of his second day. After that (with your clipboard on your knees) read out Ephesians 3:14–19 and do what he suggests.

GOOD NEWS ABOUT LOVING, LIVING AND WORTH

'What a git!' people say half-jokingly about a person who has been silly. I used to say it myself, sometimes. Until I looked it up in the dictionary to find out what it means. Git—in contemptuous use: a worthless person. I was shocked—so much that I immediately stopped using the word. It has only slipped out twice since—and now I know the meaning I am shocked all over again. No one in the whole world is worthless. I know that in my head and I know it in my heart. Every human being is enormously valuable and precious and worth more than the whole world. 'What good is it for a man to gain the whole world, yet forfeit his soul?' Jesus asked his disciples as he taught them the truth about the way things really are. 'Or what can a man give in exchange for his soul?' (Mark 8:36–37). And the soul is the true self, the person who God has created us to be (and will redeem us to be) in a relationship of love with himself.

But there are many people who do not feel valuable or precious, either to God or to anyone else. They feel worthless. The good news is that God in Christ can set them free from their sense of worthlessness—so that in deep delight they know the truth of what God said through the prophet Isaiah: 'Fear not, for I have redeemed you; I have summoned you by name; you are mine. When you pass through the waters, I will be with you... Since you are precious and honoured in my sight and because I love you' (Isaiah 43:1–4). The whole of that passage is part of the group material for this week. Also this week the contributors help us to become aware of the presence of God with us, and to find out more about the quality of the life and the love that he gives to us.

Week 5 / Sunday

Phil Lawson-Johnston

Jeremiah 31:3–4; Zephaniah 3:16–17 (NIV)

Phil Lawson-Johnston is a glass engraver and a musician. He engraves anything from two initials on a glass for a wedding anniversary to a big design on a table or a door. He also writes music and plays it. For fifteen years his group, Cloud, was based at Holy Trinity, Brompton, in London and travelled round to different places leading worship and leading celebrations. Now he lives in Oxford, occasionally tours with a team (Chris Bowater, Dave Hadden, Wes Sutton and Mark Storey) and writes and records albums. *Father of Compassion* has just been released.

Phil and I are very aware that many people suffer terribly from their lack of self-worth—and we are working together on a book that we are hoping and praying will lead them out of their sense of worthlessness into an awareness of their enormous value and preciousness to God. Phil will do a music cassette to go with it—and there will be Bible meditations on it as well. BRF hope to publish it in October, 1994.

On the subject of self-worth, Phil knows what he is talking about. 'I was the youngest of a family of five,' he told me, 'and I was very much at the tail end of the family. So I was brought up with a sense of other, big characters ahead of me—and for a long time I found it very difficult to think that I had any opinion of my own that was worth listening to.

'Through most of my teens I was very image-conscious. I tried to create an image that would make people interested in me—and I suppose that betrayed my lack of self confidence. That was back in the early 1970s, and I got involved in the drug and rock culture. In those days the culture that surrounded the type of music and the drugs included setting oneself apart from other people, and thinking oneself more perceptive and more interesting than those who didn't participate.

'It was all to do with searching for some way in which I could establish myself as being someone to whom other people might pay some attention. Someone whom others might think was important and interesting—and who they might want to know and talk to. But it didn't lead anywhere, and the idea of setting yourself apart in superior terms only succeeded in alienating people.

'Then I was introduced to the idea of Jesus being someone who wanted to get to know me as a friend and as a companion—and that was when it all began to shift around. Through the period when I first made a commitment, and subsequently experienced something of the power of the Holy Spirit to change one's life, the whole idea of having to create an image to impress others dropped away. And I really found freedom to be myself.

'I began to realize that I was important to God just as I was. I didn't have to try to be someone else. I didn't have to put forward some sort of image. What really impressed God was being myself—and that would allow him to change me and strengthen me and then hopefully to use me in some sort of way.'

'But if it was important to God for you to be you,' I said to Phil, 'then why did you have to let him change you? What needed to be changed?'

'Well, sin, basically,' said Phil. 'There were certain parts of my lifestyle which had to change fairly quickly. And they did. And other things just dropped off. One of the first things was smoking. I had been smoking quite heavily since I was 16—and when this happened I was 21. I remember wanting to give up but not being able to. I hadn't got the strength.

'Then I asked God to do it for me. I asked him really to give me a disgust for cigarettes so that it would be easier to give up. Which is exactly what happened. One night I had this packet of cigarettes in my hand and it I was so disgusted by it that I tore the whole lot up and threw it away. And I made a covenant promise to God that I would never touch another—which could have been quite rash. But from that moment all the withdrawal and everything just disappeared. Everything. That was just a small thing. But it was important at the time to see the reality that God could change me—and that he could replace something that I was relying on.

'Another thing that changed was my attitude to other people, because I became increasingly more accepting of them even when their particular image was one that I didn't go for. That was a complete contrast to the way I'd been before. I had despised people who didn't think in the same way as I did—so that really was a change for the better.

'But the biggest change was in the music. In between the period when I made a commitment to follow Jesus and when the real change took place—when I experienced the power of the Spirit—in that period I was writing songs and secretly wanting to express something about Jesus. That's what I really wanted to do because I knew in the back of my mind that Jesus was the answer. But I found it difficult to sing directly about him because I found it embarrassing.

'I also found it difficult and embarrasing to talk to others about him. But the week after I prayed for God's Holy Spirit to come in and fill me—literally that week—I wrote my first overtly Christian song. And from that moment there was just a flood of songs for about a year and a half. They weren't very good songs. But it was a good process for me, and I was learning how to express all the feelings that were inside me.'

'Why do you think you are valuable to God?' I asked Phil. 'Why do you think you have any worth?'

'First and foremost because of what is said in the Bible. About him loving us all enough to die for us. That is the obvious thing—and the greatest thing. But I am constantly being reminded of it in practical terms. Through the way that prayer does seem to work—and God does seem to respond—sometimes even to the smallest thing. Showing that he does care and that he does love.

'I have probably become even more aware of our enormous preciousness to God since I've become a parent. When I begin to analyse my feelings towards my children as a father, then my understanding of God's parenthood, and the way that he sees us as his children, has really leapt ahead.

'When I look at my children, and imagine what I would be prepared to do for them in an emergency, it gives me a glimpse into what God was prepared to do for us in an emergency—which was to send Jesus to die for us. It was a pretty extreme thing to do. But when you have got your own children you begin to understand that sort of love, because you realize what lengths you would go to in order to save them and protect them.'

Now I just wanted two more things from Phil. The Bible passage that summed up what he had just said to me—and a way for a person to pray if they don't have very much sense of their own value and preciousness to God.

'The way I have seen God reach people who are in that sort of position is primarily through song,' he said. 'Certain songs have been used which I have sung to them, and it is quite clear that God has used the words to speak to them. Some of the songs are in prayer form, and there is one in particular.

Show me dear Lord how you see me through your eyes
So that I can realise your great love for me.
Teach me O Lord that I am precious in your sight,
That as a Father loves his child so you love me.

I am yours because you have chosen me.
I am your child because you have called my name.
And your steadfast love will never change.
I will always be your precious child.

Show me dear Lord that I can never earn your love,
That a gift cannot be earned only given.
Teach me O Lord that your love will never fade
That I can never drive away your great mercy

Andy Park, copyright © 1989 Mercy Publishing. Administrated by Thank You Music.

'One of the Bible passages which seems to speak to people is in Jeremiah. It isn't a prayer, but it is a statement from God ...'

I have loved you with an everlasting love; I have drawn you with loving-kindness. I will build you up again and you will be rebuilt ...

Jeremiah 31:3–4 (NIV)

'The whole process of building up is very relevant. It isn't just a snap thing of "Yes, God loves me!" In many cases you have to reverse the habit of a lifetime. The false truth has been beaten into people. Perhaps it was a parent saying, "Oh, you're useless!" Or a teacher saying, "You will never be any good." And those things are the devil's lie—that you weren't any good and you never will be any good. What God says is: "That's not true. And I have loved you. And you are precious. And I will rebuild you." There has to be a rebuilding of our thought processes. Like the renewing of our mind. But that transformation is an ongoing process.'

Do not fear, O Zion; do not let your hands hang limp. The Lord your God is with you, he is mighty to save. He will take great delight in you, he will quiet you with his love, he will rejoice over you with singing.

Zephaniah 3:16–17 (NIV)

'You delight in your children not because they are perfect—but because they are your children. You get annoyed with them when they do things that they shouldn't—and it's the same with God. But nothing will ever take away the fact that he loves us and that he delights in us.'

David Suchet

Matthew 6:25-34; Philippians 4:6-7 (NIV)

It was great to meet Poirot in the flesh—except that in real life David Suchet is much thinner, much younger, and much more attractive. He has worked in the past with the Royal Shakespare Company—playing Iago in *Othello* and Shylock in *The Merchant of Venice*, and on the day he gave me an interview he had just finished a brilliant performance in *Oleanna*.

'I won't ask you if you enjoyed it!' he said, as we shook hands in his dressing room. 'No, don't!' I said, 'I feel as if I've been wrung out. You must feel pretty shattered as well.' He did—but he came out of his role, collected mugs of tea for us, and gave his entire attention to our interview.

We talked first about how he had become a Christian. One night in a hotel bedroom in Seattle he knew that he had to read the Bible—and next day he picked out a Bible bookshop at random from the hundreds in the phone book and rang it up. Incredibly, it was just underneath his hotel. He bought his Bible and began to read it—fascinated and absorbed, and yet also in deep despair and confusion. But the God who had been drawing David to himself held on to him—and just a few months later he was baptized. After telling me the story of his conversion he told me about the two Bible passages he had chosen for our interview.

Therefore I tell you, do not worry about your life, what you will eat or drink; or about your body, what you will wear. Is not life more important than food, and the body more important than clothes? Look at the birds of the air; they do not sow or reap or store away in barns, and yet your heavenly Father feeds them. Are you not much more valuable than they? Who of you by worrying can add a single hour to his life?

And why do you worry about clothes? See how the lilies of the field grow. They do not labour or spin. Yet I tell you that not even Solomon in all his splendour was dressed like one of these. If that is how God clothes the grass of the field, which is here today and tomorrow is thrown into the fire, will he not much more clothe you, O you of little faith? So do not worry, saying, 'What shall we eat?' or 'What shall we drink?' or 'What shall we wear?' For the pagans run after all these things, and your heavenly Father knows that you need them. But seek first his kingdom and his righteousness, and all these things will be given you as well. Therefore do not worry about tomorrow, for tomorrow will worry about itself. Each day has enough trouble of its own.

Matthew 6:25–34

Do not be anxious about anything, but in everything, by prayer and petition, with thanksgiving, present your requests to God. And the peace of God, which transcends all understanding, will guard your hearts and your minds in Christ Jesus.

Philippians 4:6–7

'Well, why have I chosen this passage? It says in the small print above it (which is not actually part of the passage) *Do Not Worry*. But I have been worried ever since I became an actor. I worry about, "How good am I going to be in my role?"—though that was when I was a younger actor and I don't think that so much now. Now I say, "How true can I be in a role?" I wonder where my next job and my next penny is going to come from—and that insecurity is still with me today.

'I used to read this passage and think, "Oh, that's lovely teaching! How wonderful Jesus is!" But then I saw something tougher in it. I realized that although Jesus is kind and gentle and understanding and sympathetic he is also very demanding. And it is Jesus who actually said (and I cannot quote word for word at the moment), "There are very few that will enter. Even those who call me Lord, Lord I will not recognize."

'So what is he saying in this passage? What does he demand from us? Well, he demands from us an acknowledgement that "His grace is sufficient for me." And that leads very well into this passage about not worrying. Because Jesus doesn't talk about himself but he talks about God his Father. And the words that Jesus said were not his own words. "What I speak to you comes from my Father. What I say is not my own." He speaks from God, his Father. And these are God's words, therefore.

'All Jesus's words are God's words. Because Jesus is God and the Father is in him. And he tells us that God insists on us not worrying about what we shall wear, what we shall eat, what we shall do and how we shall survive.

'This doesn't mean that we can't plan in our own human way for tomorrow. But we must do it trusting in him, in God—the Father, the Son and the Holy Spirit.

'Now. Before Jesus died he promised us that when he died he would send us the Comforter to live in us and to be our advocate. That is why Paul demands that our bodies should be a temple in which the Holy Spirit can reside. Actually to get a clear understanding of the Trinity is very hard. But if we are to believe (as Paul believed) that God the Father, the Son and the Holy Spirit are one God, and believe that the Spirit is in us, then that means that God is in us.

'Therefore it is silly to search for a God outside of us. It is to the God within us we must look and search for and try to contact, because it is that God that Jesus said he would send to us.

'He is here and he is part of us. Then I go back and I read God's command in the Old Testament: "Lean not on your own understanding." Once again. "Trust in him." And Jesus tells us that the two greatest commandments are that you shall love God with all your heart and with all your mind and with all your soul and with all your strength—and love your neighbour as yourself.

'When you put together some of the things that Jesus taught, what he is saying is, "You have got to trust in God. And because of the Holy Spirit you must trust that he is in you. You must give your trust to him. Don't feel separated from him. And know that every single minute of your life you are being cared for."

'And that's lovely to read and it's lovely to think about. And the God in you is lovely to be aware of. And after prayer sometimes (when I can manage to pray which I don't on a daily basis but when I can) I will try and just think about God and just welcome him into my life. "But why should I do that, though", I say. "He's in me. Why should I try and welcome him in?" And then I'm separating myself from him and so I try and come back. And I read this passage and I feel great and happy. And I get in the car and then I explode because somebody nearly crashes into me. I fail as soon as I start!

'So I have not yet learned to stop worrying—about my children or my wife or where my next bread is coming from. And as much as I adore this passage—and it gives me terrific comfort to read it—perhaps my biggest failing of all is that I cannot let the worrying go and do what what he said.

'In Luke's version of this passage Jesus says, "Do not be afraid, little flock, for your Father has been pleased to give you the kingdom. Sell your possessions and give to the poor. Provide purses for yourselves that will not wear out, a treasure in heaven that will not be exhausted, where no thief comes near and no moth destroys. For where your treasure is, there your heart will be also" (Luke 12:32–34, NIV).

'I think as human beings living in the twentieth century that is something we come up against daily. Where is our heart? We know where we would like it to be—or I know where I would like mine to be. But so often I can only find it in that place when I put myself in a situation of calm, of peace, of prayer and of meditation. Then I can allow myself to feel that I am in his presence and he is in me.

'Then I go out to the world as an actor, and I go off to rehearsals or I go off to a film studio, or I do this or I do that, and it is so hard to hang on to that which I want to hang on to. Sometimes, sometimes yes! Sometimes! And it is because of those wonderful times that I am aware of separating myself from him rather than hanging on to him.

'God will never leave me. I know that! I know that! I am taught that! But it doesn't mean I never feel it. And if I am to be real and honest about it then I must own to finding it very difficult. At the same time I go to God asking his forgiveness—and I know that I am forgiven even before I need to ask. But I do ask all the same, and I have the assurance that I am forgiven.

'But I am learning! I am learning more and more that the Holy Spirit is in me—and trusting more and more. And in certain situations I'm learning just to be calm for a second, to touch him within me, and let him guide what I say. And it is a hard lesson to learn. And who knows, maybe one day I will learn how to do it and how to give everything that I have away. Not in purely physical terms necessarily, but certainly psychologically. So that I can let go. And not only let him reside in me but really let him move me. That to me is what this section is saying.

'Trust me. Trust me. Trust me. Let go. Stop worrying. Let go!'

The Revd Ian Kitteringham

John 10:7-10, 14-15 (RSV)

Ian Kitteringham is a parish priest—and a superb one. It was Ian who encouraged me to go into the ministry myself, and, as best I can, I have tried to follow in his footsteps. He is a great listener and a great pastor. He encourages people to talk about everything—even their doubts. And in the talking about them their doubts get smaller and their faith gets bigger.

Some people thought his way of running a parish rather outmoded. 'He does what!?' exclaimed an astonished high-up in the diocese who was marginally involved with my own training. 'Visits,' I said again. 'He visits the people who live in his parish. And he talks to them. And he listens to them.' The diocesan high-up couldn't quite handle this approach so the subject was changed. But not my mind.

I still don't know of any better way of sharing the Christian faith or encouraging Christian believers than by spending time with them. And the blessing isn't just one-way—it's two-way. Whenever the parish is getting on top of him, Ian says that the best thing he can do is to go out and visit someone. Then the fire kindles again.

The passage that Ian selected was in John chapter 10. 'I picked it because it's so positive,' he said to me. 'It doesn't talk about just getting by, or being miserable, or how tough it is to be a Christian. It talks about abundant life—and I think that's lovely. Abundant life is to do with discovering a purpose and meaning in life, and discovering that life really is good. We don't need drugs to have abundant life. We can have a sense of being fulfilled, and it's exciting and it's enriching. It's not about needing artificial stimulants just to get us by. It's about really living—"the life that is life indeed."'

Truly, truly, I say to you, I am the door of the sheep. All who came before me are thieves and robbers; but the sheep did not heed them. I am the door; if any one enters by me, he will be saved, and will go in and out and find pasture. The thief comes only to steal and kill and destroy; I came that they may have life, and have it abundantly . . .

I am the good shepherd; I know my own and my own know me, as the Father knows me and I know the Father; and I lay down my life for the sheep.

'The key to that passage is the bit about the good shepherd laying down his life for the sheep. I see that as meaning that Jesus enables us to have a relationship with God. Whatever may be hopeless about our lives, and however many times we may have gone off after crazy things, nevertheless he—because he gives his life for us—tells us that nothing of that can separate us from discovering this abundant life.

'It's to do with his love and his forgiveness, and having received and accepted that then it makes life terrific. It's a very carefree life in many ways, because we aren't looking over our shoulder all the time worrying about things going wrong and the fact that we are not living up to the mark. We know we've failed in that respect, and that it still doesn't prevent him from loving us. In fact it was for this purpose that he came. To love us—and to forgive us.

'Forgiveness seems to enable us to live much more spontaneously and joyfully. We aren't taking our own temperature all the time to see how we're developing morally or spiritually—because we know that we have been forgiven and that Christ died for us. That gives us the confidence to go on and to try and live positively and lovingly, without the fear that we might be slipping up all the time.

'It stops us being self-regarding, and with any luck it means that we are better able to respond to people's demands on us—because we aren't putting our own demands in the way all the time. We aren't thinking about ourselves so much because we know that's taken care of. So we are free from our self. And we aren't afraid that if things go wrong and we let the side down then we'll be drummed out of the team.

'We've failed before, and we're going to fail again, but that doesn't mean we're weighed down with a great load of remorse and guilt. We've got a freedom to experiment, and to try and meet people where they are—in our weakness.

'We know that we haven't got much to offer, but we also know that just as Jesus says he encounters us in our weakness, so he will encounter other people in theirs. It means we aren't afraid of meeting people, either weak or strong, nor so worried by their difficulties or jealous at their success that we try to put them down.

'This is where I am conscious of the Holy Spirit, and time after time I find my experience vindicated in other people's experience. That when we feel we have come to a dead end, if in that moment we are prepared to open up to God and admit our weakness and our sense of being totally at the end of our human resources, then again and again a door seems to open.

'So abundant life is living for the present moment, confident that this is God's moment and that something will come out of it—however impossible it may seem. Then we can just let life come at us, in a prayer of complete confidence and trust.'

A prayer of abandonment

Into your hands I commend my spirit. Whatever you do I can trust you, and whatever happens I shall thank you, knowing that you have redeemed it.

The Revd David Winter

Matthew 28:16–20 (NIV)

David Winter used to be the head of religious broadcasting at the BBC. Now he is the Priest in Charge of Ducklington, in Oxfordshire, and in the few spare hours that running a parish leaves him he writes books and does various radio programmes for the BBC and Radio Oxford.

He is a great communicator—and you will probably have heard him on 'Thought for the Day' and on 'Prayer for the Day'. He talks about the things people are really doing and really concerned with, and just sometimes he gets acid letters from offended Christian listeners.

The vitriol dripped recently after a brilliant 'Thought for the Day' on how marvellous love is—sexually, emotionally and spiritually—when you have made a real commitment to your partner. But David had dared to talk about condoms in the same few minutes that he talked about Christ, and (for the pitiable few) this was outrageous.

For the rest of us it was superb, and totally biblical. Because the Bible invariably talks about the world as it is—not a Mary Poppins world where nothing really naughty or nasty ever happens.

In the real world people get very busy, and because the title of this book is *Lent for Busy People*, David said that he would like to talk about the Practice of the Presence of God. 'There are lots of passages about it,' he said, 'and my key one is the end of Matthew.'

Then the eleven disciples went to Galilee, to the mountain where Jesus had told them to go. When they saw him, they worshipped him; but some doubted. Then Jesus came to them and said, 'All authority in heaven and on earth has been given to me. Therefore go and make disciples of all nations, baptising them in the name of the Father and of the Son and of the Holy Spirit, and teaching them to obey everything I have commanded you. And surely I am with you always, to the very end of the age.'

'Some years ago I was asked to do a modern version of Brother Lawrence's *The Practice of the Presence of God*. I had never really read it—and I was amazed to find that there was this monk from the seventeenth century who had a way of looking at the presence of God which was quite unlike anything I had come across before.

'In the monastic tradition you withdraw and you seek peace and quiet—and I had always known that in my busy life I couldn't do that. There was no way that I could take a weekend at a monastery and have three hours a day of solitary contemplation. But here was Brother Lawrence saying, "No, no, that isn't the idea at all! That's a misunderstanding. It isn't that you have to withdraw from these things in order to meet with God. God is in them."

'Lawrence worked in the kitchen of a monastery—and he was only a brother, not a full monk. But what people noticed was that in his very busy and hardworking life he seemed to be stiller and to have more serenity than the monks who spent hours and hours in the contemplation of God.

'So I believe that Lawrence has got a message that is very, very relevant to modern Christians. The way we live in the modern world makes it very hard to live a "spiritual" life, because the very processes of life are dehumanizing—with machines replacing hands, computers replacing minds, and psychotherapy replacing prayer.

'These things aren't bad in themselves. But they match the accelerating advance of science, and the accelerating tempo of life, and the external tensions of events all around us. They produce a society which seems to have very little time for anything—certainly very little for making space for God.

'Yet here was Lawrence saying, "No, no! You don't make space for God. That is a complete misunderstanding. God is *in* the space." And the thing that really helped me was that you could turn (or translate) pressure into presence.

'When we are under pressure we all know that the best thing that can happen to us is to have some supportive company. To have someone we get on with coming and helping us. It may be a wife, a husband, a friend, or a colleague. And when they are there we don't feel beleaguered. The pressure hasn't stopped—but now someone is sharing it with us.

'That is exactly what God offers. That kind of presence. But—and this is what I learned from Brother Lawrence—it has to be practised. You are not just instantly and immediately aware of it. You have to remind yourself about it—and discover and experience that in the pressurized situation, in these irritating people, in this overwhelming tension, God is in it. Not apart from it.

'You don't have to pull out of it all in order to find God. He is there in the middle of it. You can find, as Lawrence did, an inner pool of something that is remarkably like tranquillity.

'That really is good news for busy people. That when you are very tense it is possible to become still—really in just in a moment.

'It is interesting to me in this Matthew passage that Jesus came and stood among them—and they worshipped him, although some doubted. Then he gave them an enormous job to do.

' "Go and make disciples of all the nations." But he says, "It's OK, because I'm with you." He wasn't saying, "Go and contemplate your navels on the side of the Mount of Olives" He gave them a job to do—and then said, "But I'm coming with you." '

Bishop Michael Turnbull

2 Timothy 1:6–7 (NEB)

Michael Turnbull is the Bishop of Rochester and he has been closely connected with the Bible Reading Fellowship for over twenty years. First as a member of the Council, then as Chairman of the Executive, and since 1989 as Chairman of the Council. He has also been Chairman of the College of Preachers since 1990. He has written *God's Front Line* (1979), *Parish Evangelism* (1980) and *Learning to Pray* (1981).

I walked up past the ancient Cathedral, with its mellow stone walls basking in the autumn sunshine, and arrived at Bishopscourt. Michael Turnbull opened the door and welcomed me in to his study. He set us up with coffee, found a plug for my tape recorder, and we began.

'I have got a favourite Bible passage,' he said to me, 'and it's 2 Timothy 1:6 and 7. Paul is writing to young Timothy to try to encourage him, and in the previous verses he has gone into a little bit of his past— talking about his grandmother and his mother. But then he turns to look at Timothy and his future.'

Michael Turnbull read out the passage from the Bible that was open on his knees:

That is why I now remind you to stir into flame the gift of God which is within you through the laying on of my hands. For the Spirit that God gave us is no craven spirit [sometimes that is translated as 'a spirit of fear'] but one to inspire strength, love and self-discipline. So never be ashamed of your testimony to our Lord.

'That passage has good memories for me. I was speaking at Scargill House, and at the end of the conference a man called Bernard Jacob gave me a book just to say "thank you". He wrote part of this passage at the front of it—and over the years he became one of my very closest friends and spiritual mentors.

'For a time our conversations (as I used him as a sort of spiritual guru) all began from this passage. So some of my own self-perceptions about the spiritual inheritance that I had, and the things that are worth reaching for in a spiritual pilgrimage, are contained in it.

'One of the things that I turn to this passage for again and again is a reminder that any spiritual ambitions that we have are total gifts. It was Bernard who helped me to understand that—and I do need reminding about it. Because at heart I really am a striver and an achiever. I plan things and I get things done and I find satisfaction in that—whether it is people being helped or programmes being launched. Whatever.

'But Bernard helped me to see that the heart of the Christian life is about receiving—and I found that a release. It links with the fact that the Spirit that we are given is not a spirit of fear.

'We all have our dark sides, and part of my dark side is that the achiever within me is bred of fear. Bernard helped me to have that self-perception: to see that you are always wanting to achieve because you are wanting to prove something about yourself—and particularly to yourself. To prove that you can actually do this—whatever it happens to be.

'That leads along a dark path, because if you fail (as frequently happens), or if you don't achieve as much as you wanted to, then you have a very poor sort of self-perception.

'Bernard threw me back to the passiveness of true Christianity—and when I come back to that I find a tremendous release. When I get anxious, or feel oppressed or overburdened or overworked, I come back to that passiveness again and again. Then it is sheer release and the fear goes. The sense of "I have to do this in order that there can be some success around" disappears.'

'So when you are wanting to get things done it's not about other people loving you,' I said, 'and it's not about other people admiring you. It's about your own desire for achievement?'

'I think it's a bit of both. I think I feel that in order for other people to approve of me then I have got to earn their approval. I can see it in myself even now, and those who are close to me tell me that I am proud of a full diary—which is an awful thing to be, isn't it? And perhaps to have a full diary is a way in which I seek approval from other people— because if my diary is full then I think that somehow I am doing things for them. But that sort of hyperactivity is a sin, and there is a darkness there...'

Michael Turnbull isn't the only one who is a striver and an achiever at heart. Even when God gives us a new heart and puts a new spirit within us we still have to resist the temptation to turn back into our old ways— whatever our own weakness happens to be. So I asked him what a good way might be to pray about this particular character tendency. I wondered if people might approach it by settling themselves down to reflect on this issue of passivity, and of receiving rather than achieving, and delighting in gift.

'Yes,' he said, 'That's a good avenue to follow. Some of my spiritual roots are very much in the evangelical mould. I am grateful for that, and I wouldn't have had it any other way. But I think that the evangelicalism that I learned as a student actually played into some of the weaknesses in myself, and my tendency to be an achiever.

'In spite of the evangelical emphasis on grace by faith alone they actually made Christian discipleship into a whole set of works. I got trapped in that in my prayer life, for instance. There was no way in which you ever thought you had done enough praying. Therefore guilt starts to build up, and you have a poor perception of yourself before God.

'You think "I am not praying enough, so I am not pleasing him. Therefore he is not going to do things for me." It's a sort of bargaining with God—and it's a hopelessly wrong way of looking at it. It's an upturning of the whole covenant principle.

'So in the last ten years or so I think perhaps I have found release in simply not worrying too much: certainly not worrying about how much work I put into prayer. I still use lists, but I don't think I am a slave to them. And if I don't get through a list when I should have done (according to what I had planned) that doesn't matter.

'Another thing is that I am happy for God to take me in prayer into highways and byways which I haven't planned. That has been a tremendous release. Not to worry if the borderline between daydreaming and true receiving sometimes gets a bit blurred. And not to think that daydreaming is necessarily wrong. It is some- times in that subconscious part of ourselves that God can get through to us. It comes back again to receiving from God. As I said, to me that is right at the heart of the gospel. It has been done for me—and I receive. Then discipleship (or achieving) arises, not out of a sense of heavy duty, but out of a joyful, thankful heart.'

Len Murray

Isaiah 58:6–10 (RSV)

The Right Hon Lord (Len) Murray of Epping Forest was General Secretary of the Trades Union Congress from 1973 to 1984. Then he took early retirement to involve himself in a range of voluntary activities. He is a governor of the Prison Service Trust and involved with Crisis at Christmas. He minds passionately about social justice, and believes that God also minds about it—and that is what the passage he has chosen is about.

Is not this the fast that I choose: to loose the bonds of wickedness, to undo the thongs of the yoke, to let the oppressed go free, and to break every yoke? Is it not to share your bread with the hungry, and bring the homeless poor into your house; when you see the naked, to cover him, and not to hide yourself from your own flesh? Then shall your light break forth like the dawn, and your healing shall spring up speedily; your righteousness shall go before you, the glory of the Lord shall be your rear guard. Then you shall call, and the Lord will answer; you shall cry, and he wil say, Here I am.

If you take away from the midst of you the yoke, the pointing of the finger, and speaking wickedness, if you pour yourself out for the hungry and satisfy the desire of the afflicted, then shall your light rise in the darkness and your gloom be as the noonday.

'I am not a theologian, but it seems to me that what God is talking about in this passage is his relationship with his people and their relationship with each other—and about the interdependence between the two.

'He's telling us what he expects of us. He expects us to do his will and to hold fast to his covenant. But he is setting out the contrast between ritual observances on the one hand, which are not in themselves adequate, and practical help on the other, and he's spelling out to us the meaning of what he means by sacrifice.

'Sacrifice is essentially to put yourself and your own self-interest second. This is what first hits me about the passage. There is such a contrast with the current ideology, which says that the greatest good is the pursuit of self-interest—and says it so strongly that it has almost been raised to the level of a moral imperative.

'God sets out in surprisingly clear terms what he expects us to do— and when he spoke through Isaiah he was often much more clear than when he spoke through the mouth of Jesus. It's put very sharply indeed here in the Old Testament.

'God expects us to deal justly, to support the oppressed, to feed the hungry, to help the homeless. He is spelling these out as our duties, and he emphasizes the positive nature of these actions and activities. It is not just a matter of expiation and of assuaging our guilt. He is saying, "This process cleanses you. This process makes the relationship between us better, and it is a form of adoration in itself."

'He is also saying here (and generally through the passage, before and afterwards) that he will help to keep us going. When we are doing these things and getting stuck into them, then he will give us strength.

'He is warning about failures (and this is more clear in chapter 57 than this one) and saying that even when we are weak and let him down he is there to give us a hand, and to bear us up.'

Because of the iniquity of his covetousness I was angry, I smote him, I hid my face and was angry; but he went on backsliding in the way of his own heart. I have seen his ways, but I will heal him; I will lead him and requite him with comfort.

Isaiah 57:17–18 (RSV)

A way to pray

To find out what God wants you to do, first you've got to listen . . .
'God, give me the power to stop talking and to listen to you.'

Second, you've got to be personal . . . 'I know that you're talking to me, and this is for me and not somebody else.'

So be quiet and listen.

'Do that which lieth nearest to thy hand and do it with all thy might.'

O God, please give me the strength to keep at it and to stick at it . . . and let it not be just a flash in the pan.

Canon W.H. Vanstone

John 12:20-28 (RSV)

Canon Vanstone wrote two fascinating books called *Love's Endeavour, Love's Expense* (which won the Collins Religious Book Award) and *The Stature of Waiting*. A parish priest for many years, Bill Vanstone is also a theologian, and he makes connections between God and all the things that happen to us in our lives. He makes theological sense of love, suffering and death—which is what Jesus was talking to his disciples about in the days before he died.

Among those who went up to worship at the feast were some Greeks. So these came to Philip, who was from Bethsaida in Galilee, and said to him, 'Sir, we wish to see Jesus.' Philip went and told Andrew; Andrew went with Philip and they told Jesus. And Jesus answered them, 'The hour has come for the Son of man to be glorified. Truly, truly, I say to you, unless a grain of wheat falls into the earth and dies, it remains alone; but if it dies, it bears much fruit. He who loves his life loses it, and he who hates his life in this world will keep it for eternal life. If any one serves me, he must follow me; and where I am, there shall my servant be also; if any one serves me, the Father will honour him.

'Now is my soul troubled. And what shall I say? "Father, save me from this hour"? No, for this purpose I have come to this hour. Father, glorify thy name.' Then a voice came from heaven, 'I have glorified it, and I will glorify it again.'

'There is a tendency to think that the suffering of Jesus was his way into glory; to believe that he suffered and that then he was glorified and invested with grandeur and splendour as a reward for what he suffered.

'But that is to miss the point, which is that the manner in which Jesus went into his passion was *itself* his glorification ... because in the time of his passion he *expended* himself, in order that man might come to understand the likeness of God, and might understand that God gives *himself* for the good of the world.

'So the glory that is properly associated with Jesus' passion is not some kind of reward. Instead, it is to be understood as the disclosure of what the presence of God is really like—the glory, or the *"shekinah"*, as they used to say in the old days, which marks the presence of God.

'That glory is not a matter of trumpets and gold and silver, the sort of physical glory with which human beings both maintain and advertise their power. Rather it is the moral glory of giving oneself for the sake of others. And so the glory of God is present actually in the figure of the crucified.

'It is not the case that first of all the crucified is humiliated and that then he is rewarded with a kind of physical splendour. The truth is rather that we have to change our perceptions, and to understand that the only glory which really counts is the moral glory of giving oneself for the being and for the good of others.

'The glorification of Jesus is therefore that utmost kind of generosity, that utmost kind of courage, that utmost kind of self-expenditure which consists in giving oneself for others, and this is true glory.

'There is not anything that can reward that sort of glory. Either you see it as being the ultimate thing, that before which we all bow down, or you do not. The glorification of Jesus is in his being lifted up as a helpless, self-giving, all-loving person: and that is the glory.

'Until one has appreciated this, until one has gone through the moral change of seeing that that which is of ultimate worth is the self-giving itself, and not some kind of reward which comes from it, then one has not really understood.

'But perhaps in ordinary life we do in a way see this. There are certain people who so give themselves for others, or give themselves for some noble cause, that we say, "I wish I had been that person"—and then our moral sense is coming into play, and we are recognizing that there is nothing more compelling, nothing more truly honourable and adorable, than that kind of bold and generous self-expenditure, which says, "I am for you, I am for others", and which seeks no reward.

'Reward is a trivial thing—of whatever it may consist, whereas the nobility of that kind of self-giving which says, "I will expend myself for you, my dear, and I hold nothing back"—that is the glorification of Jesus.'

A way to pray

So perhaps the appropriate prayer with which to end these simple thoughts is this: Oh God, give me the courage and the generosity to expend myself for the good of that which is not myself. Help me to see that in this lies the true glory ... not in becoming well known, or becoming possessed of the world's glory, but in expending myself in the ultimate courage and the ultimate generosity and the ultimate nobility in which I say: 'Here am I, make me available for what is required for the service and the sake of others.'

Material for reflection and groups

Talk about our worth and value to God as the Bible and as this week's contributors talk about it.

Talk about the presence of God as The Revd David Winter and Brother Lawrence describe it.

Talk about the self-giving of God as Jesus described it and as Canon W.H. Vanstone comments on it.

Finish by using the song on page 88 of Phil Lawson-Johnston's piece as a prayer. Then, as we move towards Holy Week, read out John 12:20–28 from Canon Vanstone and then, after a few minutes of silence for reflection, use his final prayer.

GOOD NEWS FOR A BAD AND BEAUTIFUL WORLD

The Most Revd and Right Hon. George Carey, Archbishop of Canterbury

John 3:14-17; 12:31-33 (NRSV)

Yesterday we read about the grain of wheat that had to fall into the ground and die. Today, at the start of Holy Week, we look at the death that lies ahead, and at the glory and the astonishing benefits which Jesus said would flow from it. Good news for a bad, beautiful and infinitely beloved world. George Carey looks at two great passages from the Gospel of John which spell it out.

'... Now is the judgment of this world; now the ruler of this world will be driven out. And I, when I am lifted up from the earth, will draw all people to myself.' [Jesus] said this to indicate the kind of death he was to die.

And just as Moses lifted up the serpent in the wilderness, so must the Son of Man be lifted up, that whoever believes in him may have eternal life. For God so loved the world that he gave his only Son, so that everyone who believes in him may not perish but may have eternal life. Indeed, God did not send the Son into the world to condemn the world, but in order that the world might be saved through him.

'In spite of what we sometimes think as we look around—"is it possible that God still loves this world, where bad news bombards us from all sides?"—the message of the gospel is that God never gives up! He wants all people to know him—and his arms are wide open to us.

'Both these passages proclaim good news to us all! For the helpless, the poor, and the many who feel marginalized by a world that esteems wealth, success and fame as the measure of the good life, the gospel gives hope.

'It says, "God has come near to you in Jesus Christ. This life does not last for ever. But if you believe—that is 'trust in him'—then you will live for ever. That is God's offer to you."

'But it is also an offer and a gift to all of us. We don't have to be poor and afflicted to know the wonderful truth that God is for us and loves us.

'As we look out on a world which shows obvious strains of man's insatiable appetite for the good life, John 12 tells us that God will overcome all enemies which resist his loving control. When Christ died on the cross—when he was lifted up—the ruler of this world was judged.

'Jesus is contrasting the true ruler of the world, God, with the one who is the "usurper". The "lifting up" of Christ on the cross will be the downfall of Satan. By implication Jesus is saying that there are two ways of looking at life. First, we can see it as out of control, chaotic and on its way to destruction. Many people see life like that—they feel it is futile and purposeless.

'Or second, we can allow Christ to touch our eyes so that we can see the spiritual reality—the devil has been cast out because through Christ all things have been reconciled to God through the cross. He purchased our "peace" (Colossians 1:20).

'Today is Palm Sunday. It represents the last stage of Jesus' pilgrimage for us. Today we think of Jesus "going up" to Jerusalem. Today when Jews return to Jerusalem they talk of "going up" (*aliyah*). Jesus' "*aliyah*" was a visible one—he is lifted up for our sake.

'In both these passages from John there is a "lifting up". As Moses "lifted up the serpent" and "when I am lifted up from the earth ..." In both passages the point of being "lifted up" is so that people may see for themselves and turn to God.

'The challenge for the church and every Christian is to lift up the cross of Christ and make it so glorious that others may experience for themselves the power and love of Christ.

' "God so loved the world that he gave his only Son, so that everyone who believes in him may not perish but may have eternal life" (John 3:16). That is one of the great verses of the Bible—and I would love every reader of this book to know it by heart.

'It is wonderful news, because it sets out the offer of salvation so clearly and so simply. We see that it proceeds from God himself, that it is the gift of his Son, and that it results in the gift of eternal life.

'The marvellous thing about Christianity is that salvation is a free gift of God. We don't have to do anything to earn eternal life. It costs us nothing to possess it—though once we do possess it we discover that living out the faith will demand all we have.

'We give gifts to other people because we are already in a relationship with them. But it isn't like that with God. He makes a relationship with us by giving us the gift of life—through the death of Christ.

'The Apostle Paul wrote to the Romans that "God proves his love for us in that while we were still sinners Christ died for us . . . [and] if while we were enemies, we were reconciled to God through the death of his Son, much more, surely, having been reconciled, will we be saved by his life" (Romans 5:8–10).'

A prayer

Lord, thank you for sending your Son
to make sense of this crazy, broken world.
I do trust you.
Walk with me into this new day—
as I enter into the risk of living—
as I seek to share the gospel: that
'God so loved the world
that he gave his only Son,
so that everyone who believes in him
may not perish but may have eternal life.'
May I lift up the cross
through the quality of the life that I live
as well as through the words that I say.

Holy Week / Monday

Sir Harry Secombe

John 14:1–4 (AV)

Let not your heart be troubled: ye believe in God, believe also in me. In my Father's house are many mansions: if it were not so, I would have told you. I go to prepare a place for you. And if I go and prepare a place for you, I will come again, and receive you unto myself, that where I am, there ye may be also. And whither I go ye know, and the way ye know.

Harry Secombe describes himself as actor, comedian and singer—in that order. When he talked to me he was appearing in *Pickwick*—with the star part, and he fitted the character like a glove. Larger than life, immensely warm-hearted, and enormously popular.

He is well known on television for his programme *Highway* and on radio for *The Goon Show*. He used to write regularly for *Punch* and for *The Times Literary Supplement*, and he has also written various books: they include *The Harry Secombe Diet Book* and his autobiography, *Arias and Raspberries*.

His sense of humour is irrepressible. Right at the start of our interview I said, 'Where shall I begin?', at which he burst into song in his superb tenor: 'Where shall I begin...?' So we began with laughter, which was a good starting place.

Harry Secombe has sung since he was a small boy. He was a choirboy in Swansea from the age of seven, and the Bible passage he had chosen dated from then.

'We used to sing anthems,' he told me, 'and there was one that stuck in my mind. "Let not your heart be troubled... believe in me." It used to come into my head quite often when we were in action during the war in North Africa—and it always stuck there. It was a comfort and a solace in a rather frightening world. Because it says, "Let not your heart be troubled... in my Father's house are many mansions." That meant a lot to me.

'When I started doing *Highway* I met so many people whose faith was very strong and who had come through tremendous ordeals in their life, and that belief was the cornerstone of their faith.'

'It's a marvellous passage, isn't it?' I said. 'Yes. When things are hard you can get a lot of comfort from it—and I think the older you get the more comfort you need.'

'Do you believe in the resurrection?' I questioned. 'Of course I do!' he said, with deep feeling. Then I asked what he thought Jesus meant when he said that he was going to prepare a place for us, and that he would come again and take us to be with him.

'I think it means that if you believe you go to be with God when you die. I'm not naïve enough to think that you'll live on a cloud strumming away to God with a long white beard. There is a passage in one of Rupert Brooke's poems that says,

> And think this heart, all evil shed away,
> A pulse in the eternal mind, no less,
> Gives somewhere back the thoughts by England given.

'That's a marvellous thought,' he said. 'I once had a chat with the Archbishop of Canterbury, Robert Runcie, and I mentioned those words to him. He nodded very wisely and said, "How true that is." '

Then I asked Sir Harry how he prays. 'I'm not so good in my own words,' he said, 'For me it's a mental communication rather than a spoken one. But there is one prayer—and it's a great one for these days.'

A prayer

O Lord, support us all the day long, until the shadows lengthen
and the evening comes, and the busy world is hushed, and the
fever of life is over, and our work is done. Then, Lord, in your
mercy grant us a safe lodging, a holy rest, and peace at the last,
through Jesus Christ our Lord.

Susan Howatch

Romans 8:28 (AV)

Susan Howatch's series of brilliant novels about the Church of England are compulsive and fascinating reading. 'One of the most original novelists writing today,' said *Cosmopolitan*, and Andrew Greeley of the *Washington Post* wrote that 'Susan Howatch may well become the Anthony Trollope of the 20th century. Howatch is more than just a novelist of ideas ... She is a skilled storyteller who makes the reader wonder and care about her people.'

Glittering Images was the first in the series, and *Mystical Paths* the fifth. 'Ask her when the last one is coming out,' friends said to me eagerly (and rather enviously) when they discovered that I was going to see her. She was in fact still writing it when she agreed to give me an interview—and the theological point that she is working out in it is the one which she talked to me about. The astonishing truth of Paul's statement in Romans 8:28:

...we know that all things work together for good to them that love God...

'In the early 1980s my daughter had gone to live with my husband in America,' she told me. 'But it didn't work out. It was a disaster and

110

finally when she fell ill I brought her back to England for treatment. Her complete recovery was not in doubt but it took many months, and this was a difficult time for both of us.'

'Eventually, she got well enough to want to resume her education, and that meant we had to move. Because she was in the American education system she had to go to an American school in London. I had already moved twice, and this would mean that I was going to have to move three times in two years.

'I was very happy that she was better. But I was just so exhausted. I've never liked London, and I thought "Why have I got to move back to this ghastly place? And what does it all mean? And is it going to work out? And how do I stand it?"

'I looked in the paper and I saw that the new Dean of Guildford, Alex Wedderspoon, was going to preach. I love sermons. That's my thing. So I thought, "I'll cheer myself up. I'll go and hear the new Dean of Guildford preach." So I went. I went in depressed—at the end of my tether and wondering how on earth I was going to keep going. Then the Dean got up in the pulpit and he preached such a sermon! I went out of that Cathedral saying to myself, "I'll be all right now." And I was. I went out thinking I could conquer the world.

'He preached on Romans 8:28 and it was amazing. I didn't know it at all. I should have written to him, but I didn't. Then three years later, in 1990, he wrote to me out of the blue to ask if I would give a sermon to launch the book week. They were going to have a big Eucharist in the cathedral and he wanted me to preach at it. I had never preached a sermon in my life, because I never speak in public. I had to make a speech to 1,500 people when I was seventeen and afterwards I said I would never, never again speak in public! And I have kept to that.

'But when Alex asked me to preach I thought, "For him. Yes!" And when I finally met him I said, "In 1987 you saved my life. You preached on Romans 8:28." I am trying to weave what he said into my final book in the Starbridge series—*Absolute Truths*. I have had six years now to meditate on it and finally it is spewing out into my book. I have taken Alex's theme and developed it a bit further.'

I asked Susan Howatch what Alex Wedderspoon had said—and she gave me her own rendering of his sermon, vividly remembered because it had been such a turning point for her.

'He started off with "All things work together for good to them that love God." But then he said "It's not much good saying that to parents whose only child has been killed in an accident—or to someone who is dying of cancer. What a terrible thing to say. It just sounds so smug—and how could anyone say it? And how could St Paul have written it?

' "St Paul knew all about disadvantage and adversity," he said. "He was kicked all over the place and and maltreated and thrust into prison. Yet he could still come up saying that. How did he say it and what does it all mean? When the world is so full of suffering and pain, and when so many terrible things happen, how could he possibly say that all things work together for good?"

' "Well," he said, "it's really a mistranslation. The real translation is that all things *intermingle* for good for those who love God. And *intermingle* means that the bad stays bad and the good stays good. But they intermingle. So instead of all the ingredients mixing, instead of bad and good mixing up and coming up smelling wonderful, like a cake coming out of the oven, it's not like that at all.

' "The bad things stay bad. Someone is dying of cancer—and that is terrible. Dreadful. And the good things stay good. But the good things and the bad things intermingle to make a pattern, and *this* is what's important."

'He said that in the war a man called Viktor Frankl had been in a concentration camp. He was a psychiatrist, and he had discovered that people could emerge from concentration camps, and they could survive anything, so long as they thought their suffering had meaning. What destroyed people was meaningless suffering.

'So when you say that all things intermingle for good it is actually the pattern that the light makes when it interpenetrates with the dark. It is the pattern that gives these terrible things meaning.

'What we are really talking about is a very strong doctrine of redemption. How God redeems everything. The darkness it is always there—and it is dark. Dark, dark, dark. But the light is always trying to penetrate the darkness. It is the pattern of the light penetrating the darkness that gives it meaning. And it is the meaning which enables those who suffer to survive.

Meditate

Read Romans 8:28 again and meditate on it.

Susan Howatch

Romans 8:28, 35-39 (AV)

And we know that all things work together for good to them that love God, to them who are called according to his purpose...

'In 1990 I read John Polkinghorne and W.H. Vanstone, both in the same summer. I read John's trilogy (and he's written another one since then), and it was very exciting—because religion and science are now seen as complementary and not opposed to each other. Vanstone is a religious genius. Absolutely stunning.

'In *Love's Endeavour, Love's Expense* Vanstone is very adamant that God never wills suffering, but suffering is part of the creative process. You can't create without waste and tragedy and awfulness. I realize this myself as a creator. When I write a book a lot of things are wasted. Thrown in the waste paper basket, or crossings out of this, that or the other. "That is an awful lot of waste and mess," I think, "and what a lot of time I have taken." But when the printed book is finally in my hands then everything is redeemed. All the bits in the waste paper basket and all the mess. It is all redeemed. Because I could not have got to the final draft without making all the mistakes and the errors and the waste.

'This is where Polkinghorne is so good. Because he stresses that human beings are at the beginning of their journey. Humanity hasn't been going very long—but the universe has been around for fifteen billion years. So Polkinghorne gives us the divine perspective on things. God is the creator, and we have still got a long way to go on the human journey. So it's all rather a mess at the moment. But we have to concentrate on the fact that God is always working to redeem what goes wrong, and on the pattern of the light interpenetrating the darkness— and giving meaning to the darkness and to the suffering.

'When I finally met Alex in in 1990 I asked him to give me a copy of his sermon. So he did, and I often meditate on it. People will say about suffering, "It's a mystery. I don't understand it." But I don't think that's the way to carry on. That's pathetic. You've got to come up with something. Perhaps it's easier for a writer to see that the creative process generates this sort of understanding—the fact that you can't make an omelette without breaking eggs.

'Back in 1987, when I was *in extremis*, what helped me was the whole idea of intermingling. That the bad remains bad, and the good remains good, but that all the time God is working to redeem the situation. Alex had been talking about surviving, and living with suffering, and about the fact that there was meaning. He said that sometimes the meaning simply gave you the strength to go on going on. And I thought, "That's just what I need right now. Just the strength to keep on keeping on." And that's what he gave me from the pulpit. The strength to keep on keeping on when I was at a very low ebb.

'When I finally talked to Alex I said to him that it isn't just every word one has written for one book that gets redeemed. It is everything that one has ever written—because one couldn't write without all the experience that has gone before. One couldn't produce the final book without all this tremendous labour. But all the waste is redeemed by what one holds in one's arms. Like a baby. For me every single word, discarded or otherwise, has value; *all* the words used are important to me.

'So that is why Romans 8:28 has a very special meaning for me. And soon afterwards there is that marvellous passage about nothing ever being able to separate us from the love of God.'

Who shall separate us from the love of Christ? Shall tribulation, or distress or persecution, or famine, or nakedness, or peril, or sword? As it is written, For thy sake we are killed all the day long; we are accounted as sheep for the slaughter. Nay, in all these things we are more than conquerors through him that loved us. For I am persuaded, that neither death, nor life, nor angels, nor principalities, nor powers, nor things present, nor things to come, nor height, nor depth, nor any other creature, shall be able to separate us from the love of God, which is in Christ Jesus our Lord.

A footnote

What Susan Howatch had said to me (and what Alex Wedderspoon had preached) about Romans 8:28 fascinated me. It made beautiful sense. A few days later I had lunch with a man whose son had left home and gone into a very far country—stealing, sleeping around and taking drugs. Because he was a great admirer of Susan Howatch, and because he knew about our interview, I told him what she had learned from the Dean of Guildford. The man nodded. 'Yes,' he said, 'That's very good.' He wasn't being required to believe impossible things—that what his son had done was good. But if the light of God was endlessly working to penetrate the darkness then there was hope.

Then I told the same thing to a man whose son of 24 had been killed in a car crash: Tim—whom you will meet on Easter Sunday (and also in heaven). 'Yes, I like that,' said the broken-hearted father. 'The bad is still very bad, and the dark is still very dark.' It didn't take away the pain. And it didn't pretend that the darkness was light. But the redeemer God is there in the agony—just as God was in Christ, reconciling the world to himself.

The God whom I worship is one who is here with us in the midst of all our suffering—and a poem that I love by Edward Shillito sums it all up. It is called 'The prayer of a modern Thomas'.

If Thou, O God, the Christ didst leave,
In Him, not Thee, I do believe;
To Jesus dying all alone,
To His dark Cross, not Thy bright Throne,
My hopeless hands will cleave.

But if it was Thy love that died,
Thy voice that in the darkness cried,
The print of nails I long to see,
In Thy hands, God, who fashioned me.
Show me *Thy* pierced side.

A few days later I decided to look up Romans 8:28 and the words 'work together' in my concordance. The phrase is only used three times in the New Testament. In Mark 16:20 and James 2:22 as well as Romans 8:28 the Greek word is *sunergeo* (and I don't know Greek, so all I can do is look it up in concordances and dictionaries).

Interested by the fact that it is only used three times I mentioned it to Richard Fisher, who is the Chief Executive of BRF and has a degree in classics (as well as being a friend of mine). He had also been intrigued by what Susan Howatch had said, and now he said, 'Synergy! That's what it's saying.'

For me that was like being hit with a charge of electricity—except that it didn't hurt. Just flooded in even more light—and an even deeper sense of wonder at the astonishing things that God does.

Finally, at an 85th birthday party for Professor Sir Norman Anderson, I recounted these facts about Romans 8:28 over a delicious birthday lunch. John and Penny Trapnell were the hosts, and the guests of honour were Lord and Lady Coggan—the Donald Coggan who used to be Archbishop of Canterbury and is also the President of the Bible Reading Fellowship. He immediately wrote down the word *sunergeo* in his diary. Then he cross-examined our host about it.

John Trapnell is a surgeon and a scientist. 'Isn't it a scientific word?' asked Donald Coggan. 'Yes,' said John. 'Well, what does it mean?' 'It's about two substances that remain totally separate,' said John, 'but they work together and make something that's better than both of them. Like the penicillin bacillus on mould.'

The Shorter Oxford Dictonary says that synergy is the combined or correlated action of a group of bodily organs (as nerve-centres, muscles, etc.); hence, of mental faculties, of remedies, etc.

So Romans 8:28 is talking about a synergy brought about by God. He is the power that makes it happen. A divine intermingling of all things—bad and terrible things as well as good and beautiful things—to bring about an ultimate good. That really is good news for a bad and beautiful world.

Bishop Wilfred Wood

John 13:3–5; 15:9–15 (NRSV)

Wilfred Wood is the first black bishop in the Church of England. He has been Chairman of the Institute of Race Relations and is Chairman of the Martin Luther King Memorial Trust. He has a deep concern for children and for people who are badly housed and is active on their behalf, and he has written *Vicious Circle* with J. Downing. In July 1994, at the time of the Black Anglican Congress in York, BRF will publish his book, *Keep the Faith, Baby!*

Jesus, knowing that the Father had given all things into his hands, and that he had come from God and was going to God, got up from the table, took off his outer robe, and tied a towel around himself. Then he poured water into a basin and began to wash the disciples' feet and to wipe them with the towel that was tied around him...

As the Father has loved me, so I have loved you; abide in my love. If you keep my commandments, you will abide in my love, just as I have kept my Father's commandments and abide in his love. I have said these things to you so that my joy may be in you, and that your joy may be complete.

This is my commandment, that you love one another as I have loved you. No one has greater love than this, to lay down one's life for one's friends. You are my friends if you do what I command you. I do not call you servants any longer, because the servant does not know what the master is doing; but I have called you friends, because I have made known to you everything that I have heard from my Father.

Love, unity and service—the three great themes of the ministry of Jesus are his choice for humankind's conduct of our own relationships. This was never more vividly demonstrated than on that Thursday evening when he was preparing his friends for his self-offering on the following day.

He wanted them to understand this culminating act of integrity with all that he had said and done before. So he gave a new commandment (love) which would produce a new people bonded to himself (unity) and showed us how to observe it (service).

Jesus put it plainly: 'A new commandment I give you. Love one another as I have loved you.' This is love akin to the love of God himself. Love that is patient, kind and envies no one, never boastful, conceited or rude, never selfish, not quick to take offence, keeps no score of wrongs. Love that will lay down its life for its friends.

So the only law this new people of God will need is the law of this love. It comes from the mouth of God because it comes from the mouth of Jesus. And this law of love so completely fulfils God's requirement that St Paul later said, 'Owe no man anything but to love one another.' And still later St Augustine urged: 'Love God and do what you will'— knowing that anyone who does love God with the love of Jesus will do only the will of God.

This new commandment also has its special celebratory meal instituted at the same time. The ingredients are the ordinary stuff of everyday eating and drinking—bread and wine. But ordinary bread and wine when blessed by Jesus and given to his friends becomes life-giving body and blood. So Jesus takes us—ordinary people with ordinary lives—and by blessing us he raises the quality of our ordinary lives and we become life-giving to those whom we serve in his name.

In this way Christ instituted the Eucharist. For almost two thousand years since that night humankind has found no better way of celebrating both the ordinary and the extraordinary events of human existence. The Eucharist has been celebrated for kings and queens at their coronations and for criminals facing execution.

It has been celebrated with all the pomp and pageantry of a Papal Mass with hundreds of concelebrating priests, and in the shanty town hovel by the bedside of an old woman dying of cancer; on the battlefield, in the grimness of prisoner-of-war camps, in schools and hospitals.

It has been celebrated in the open air in the presence of heads of state, and secretly in underground caves by Christians hiding from the police. In great cathedrals and in people's kitchens. At marriages and funerals—the same Eucharist, the same unfailing means of remembering the presence of Christ among his people, no matter where his people happen to be. And whoever they are, and wherever they are— living or departed—we are united in the Eucharist with him and so with one another.

But in addition to a symbol of unity every people has its own way of recognizing greatness. Earthly kingdoms provide decorations, titles and honours. The people of God also have a method of identifying greatness correctly, also established on this occasion by the example of Christ himself.

He took a basin and a towel and performed the servant's job of washing the feet of honoured guests. As he did so he reminded his followers: 'You call me master and Lord, and rightly so, because that is what I am. But if I, your Lord and master, wash your feet, you also ought to wash one another's feet.'

On Christ's scale of values greatness is measured in terms of humility and service. In his kingdom the have-nots, the losers in life's rat race, those who are despised by their fellows—these are all honoured guests.

Every year I am humbly grateful to God when I have the privilege of sharing in a small representation of Christ's example. But I know that we would be making a mockery of Christ's example if our ritual feet washing on Maundy Thursday in the controlled and contrived environment of church buildings is not matched by our service to those who are hungry, homeless and jobless on the streets outside. And if such service is not offered in humility and without condescension.

Love, unity and service—God's offer made possible by the suffering and the death of Christ. May we in gratitude and humility accept that offer by loving one another as Christ loved us, by celebrating our unity in him and with one another in the sacrament of the altar, and by humble service of Christ's honoured brothers and sisters—the wretched of the earth.

The Revd Professor Leslie Houlden

Mark 14:22–25; 15:33–35, 38–39 (RSV)

Leslie Houlden is Professor of Theology at King's College, London, and the author of several Bible commentaries and books—among them *The Johannine Epistles*, *The Pastoral Epistles* and *Connections*.

He wrote:

'We hold that from the death of Jesus flow forgiveness and restoration. On this day of all days we must see that for ourselves. So we set out to see it through the story of the events surrounding the death.

'Here we listen to the story as the Gospel of Mark gives it to us. Of course the story is about Jesus, but it also includes other characters. They let us see the truth about Jesus, and about ourselves in relation to him, for we can stand in their shoes as we read and attend.

The meal points to the death (Mark 14:22–25)

And as they were eating, he took bread, and blessed, and broke it, and gave it to them, and said, 'Take; this is my body.' And he took a cup, and when he had given thanks he gave it to them, and they all drank of it. And he said to them, 'This is my blood of the covenant, which is poured out for many. Truly, I say to you, I shall not drink again of the fruit of the vine until that day when I drink it new in the kingdom of God.'

'So, first, we identify with the disciples. They are at table with Jesus. They receive his bread and his wine, and by that very act show their bond with him. Even with us, sharing a person's food and drink creates a link, much more so with them.

'Jesus calls the bread and wine his body and blood; that is, he identifies them with himself and with what will soon happen to him.

To receive this food and drink is to accept Jesus' fate. It is as good as taking up the cross with and for him (Mark 8:34; 15:21). To do this is to be a truly committed disciple. So we in the Eucharist express our commitment and avow our discipleship.

'But among the group at table is Judas the betrayer, Peter the denier— and indeed the whole bunch will soon sleep callously through Jesus' distress in the garden and at his arrest they will flee (14:50).

'What of us? Is not our discipleship, even in its most devout moments, precarious and fragile? Despite his gifts to us, is there not deep in us that which puts us among the opposition to Jesus? Is not this the truth about the human race—that in relation to us, Jesus is alone, our precious, solitary saviour, our one lifeline?'

Jesus is at one with us (Mark 15:33–35)

And when the sixth hour had come, there was darkness over the whole land until the ninth hour. And at the ninth hour Jesus cried with a loud voice, 'Eloi, Eloi,lama sabachthani?' which means, 'My God, my God, why hast thou forsaken me?' And some of the bystanders hearing it said, 'Behold, he is calling Elijah.'

'Now, second, we see the depth of his aloneness. Mysteriously, Jesus knows himself abandoned by God. How can this be? Or rather, how can it not be, if he is to give any good to us who live in this marvellous yet outrageous world, where delight and horror jostle in our lives for mastery?

'To this sombre generosity of Jesus' suffering, we can react trivially— offering, like those who stood by, the palliative drug. We can, if we choose, decline to interpret our experience profoundly, keeping it at a level of moderate misery and moderate joy. But we miss thereby the point at which God meets us.

Faith opens all doors (Mark 15:38–39)

And the curtain of the temple was torn in two, from top to bottom. And when the centurion, who stood facing him, saw that he thus breathed his last, he said, 'Truly, this man was the Son of God!'

'So, third, Jesus' death, truly accepted and looked at steadily, opens the way for us. It is like the tearing of the curtain which veils God's presence in the Temple. We can then, like the centurion, come to faith: faith which is direct, decisive, and all-encompassing.

'There is no make-believe in treading this path, no deluding rhetoric or easy optimism. To find faith through this death is to face the worst head-on—and to come forth with a new and quite different strength. Jesus' death was tragedy, and it took place in a world where for most people much of the time life is tragedy. But to us, living in such a world, it breaks in with magnificent love. Then we can see "the salvation of our God" and serve in his Kingdom.'

> O, dearly, dearly has he loved,
> And we must love him too,
> And trust in his redeeming blood,
> And try his works to do.

Easter Eve

The Revd Professor Leslie Houlden

Habakkuk 3:17–19 (RSV)

Though the fig tree do not blossom, nor fruit be on the vines, the produce of the olive fail and the fields yield no food, the flock be cut off from the fold and there be no herd in the stalls, yet I will rejoice in the Lord, I will joy in the God of my salvation. God, the Lord, is my strength; he makes my feet like hinds' feet, he makes me tread upon my high places.

'The Bible is a set of windows each giving on to a view of reality. Look through any one of them and you may perceive the whole universe in relation to God and your own place within it.

'The Bible is a means to an end. "Reality" is a two-sided word: it refers to "what there is", but it refers also to what there is taken at its sharpest, with the utmost candour, not in part or as we wish it were.

'In the Bible, some perceptions of the universe are, for good reason, partial: they give us one slant on "what there is", perhaps comforting or instructive or inspiring. They focus our eyes for the moment upon only part of what we know to be true.

'Habakkuk goes beyond these simple and straightforward reactions to human experience. His is a "worst-case scenario". Why does this passage appeal? It is because of its honesty. It stares the world, experience, and God himself full in the face. It blinks at nothing. It refuses a religion of easy consolation and trivial theologizing. It rejects salvation seen as a way of escape. It puts aside the fudging which every serious unbeliever views as the prime sin of the over-confident believer.

'Yet it also refuses the path of hesitant faith, of dignified and purist agnosticism. It combines honesty with the deepest love of God and total abandonment to him. But, however moving, is this something from which Christ has delivered us, making us more assured and joyful? I think not. The reality which faces us is, in its bafffing assemblage of delight and horror, no different from that which Habakkuk faced, Christ or no Christ.

'We know that some in earliest Christianity had a difficulty in accepting the horror of Jesus' death. Paul urged his readers to put aside a joy which was too easy or superficial; he insisted on contemplating the death of Jesus as the heart of his disclosure of God. "We preach Christ crucified, a stumbling block to Jews and folly to Gentiles..." (1 Corinthians 1:23).

'Mark too, in his Gospel, stressed above all the death of Jesus in all its realism, utterly problematic though it is. "And at the ninth hour Jesus cried... My God, my God, why hast thou forsaken me?" (Mark 15:34). Who can fathom the meaning of those words? But how dare any Christian soften them and remove their sting!

'The face of God is defined for us by what Jesus was. In his light we see the purging but assuaging light of God.'

A meditation

Imagine your life without the things you value most; and consider the lives of those who are truly up against it in one way or another. Today is Easter Eve. For the disciples the light of the world had gone out. Then, contemplating your 'worst-case scenario', read aloud Habakkuk's affirmation:

'Yet I will rejoice in the Lord,
I will joy in the God of my salvation.
God, the Lord, is my strength;
he makes my feet like hinds' feet,
he makes me tread upon my high places.'

How deep is the assurance with which you say those words? How does the reality of Jesus help you to mean them?

Tim Wright

John 6:53–59 (NIV); John 20:11–18 (NIV); Luke 21:1–7 (AV)

On a rainy September morning Tim Wright set out from Brixton in a borrowed van. He was going to collect wood from the Darvell Christian community in Robertsbridge to take to Brixton Prison, where some of the men make furniture and toys in the prison workshop. But on the way Tim's van skidded on the wet road and hit a lorry head on. He was taken to hospital and put on a life support machine, but medically speaking he was dead.

That night his parents, Pam and Michael, gave permission for his organs to be used for transplants—and the next day three operations took place. Two people were given kidney transplants and one person a heart transplant. Tim was 24 years old.

Two years before he died he had been baptized in Kensington Temple in London, where he was the drummer in one of the bands. The service had been on television, and this is part of what Tim said before he went down into the water.

'I'm a musician, and I'm shortly going to take a step to cement my commitment to God by being baptized. In a Christian family Christianity has never been anything I have been alien to, and I have always been comfortable with Christian values. But it's only now that I'm getting my confidence together. I'm not ashamed to say, "Yes, I'm a Christian!".

'It is not an easy thing to be a Christian. Look at the ridicule you get from people. They say, "You're some kind of freak. Why do you believe in all this rubbish?" If I was a weak person and easily crushed I wouldn't pick Christianity, because it's not an easy road. So many people have this ridiculous, stereotyped view of what Christians are—that they're some weird, freaking, rather wet kind of people.

'But that's not what I am! I'm a Christian because I know it's totally true ... and which one of *them* has a leader like Jesus, a leader who's still alive? Jesus is still alive—and that is all I've got to say about that!'

The Revd Colin Dye asked Tim some questions about his family and about his faith, and the final question he put to him was 'What would you say to other young people today who were thinking about accepting Jesus Christ?'

'It's totally true,' Tim replied, 'and I wouldn't see any point in living if

Jesus wasn't there, because he gives me all my hope and all my purpose for my life. I'm going to mean business with him!'

The congregation cheered and clapped. Then, as Tim was submerged in the deep water of Kensington Temple's big baptismal font, the minister said: 'Tim, on confession of your faith in the Lord Jesus and at your own request we now baptize you in the name of the Father and the Son and the Holy Spirit.'

The band started to play and the people started to sing. The hymn they sang was the one that the congregation sang at the end of the thanksgiving service for Tim's life. The last verse is an invitation and a promise.

Give your life to Jesus, let Him fill your soul,
Let Him take you in His arms and make you whole.
As you give your life to Him He'll set you free.
You will live and reign with Him eternally.

Jesus made the promise of eternal life when he was teaching by the Sea of Galilee, and he told people how he would give it to whoever wanted it:

Jesus said to them, 'I tell you the truth, unless you can eat the flesh of the Son of Man and drink his blood, you have no life in you. Whoever eats my flesh and drinks my blood has eternal life, and I will raise him up at the last day. For my flesh is real food and my blood is real drink. Whoever eats my flesh and drinks my blood remains in me, and I in him. Just as the living Father sent me and I live because of the Father, so the one who feeds on me will live because of me. This is the bread that came down from heaven. Your forefathers ate manna and died, but he who feeds on this bread will live for ever.

John 6:53–58 (NIV)

Before anyone could feed on the bread the grain of wheat had to fall into the ground and die, in the terrible crucifixion and death of Good Friday. But Good Friday wasn't the end of the story—any more than Tim's death is the end of Tim's story.

On the 8 September, the day that Tim died, his devastated parents and their three other children, Matthew, Hannah and Sam, got home from the hospital very late. Their mother opened *Living Light* for that evening, and this is what she read (and at the top of the page she has written 'Timmy with Jesus. Hold on.')

Christ rose first.

I must fall and die like a grain of wheat that falls between the furrows of the earth. Unless I die, I will be alone—a single seed. But my death will produce many new young grains—a plentiful harvest of new lives.

Christ actually did rise from the dead, and has become the first of millions who will come back to life again some day...

You have become a part of him, and so you died with him, so to speak, when he died; and now you share his new life, and shall rise as he did...

Our Saviour the Lord Jesus... will take these dying bodies of ours and change them into glorious bodies like his own, using the same mighty power that he will use to conquer all else everywhere.

He is the leader of all who rose from the dead, so that he is first in everything...

And if the Spirit of God, who raised up Jesus from the dead, lives in you, he will make your dying bodies live again after you die, by means of this same Holy Spirit living within you.

I am the one who raises the dead and gives them life again. Anyone who believes in me, even though he dies like everyone else, shall live again.

1 Corinthians 15:23; John 12:24; 1 Corinthians 15:20; Romans 6:5;

Philippians 3:20–21; Colossians 1:18; Romans 8:11; John 11:25

After the agony of Good Friday there was the glory and the wonder of Easter morning. On the third day Jesus was raised from the dead, and his astonished disciples knew that he was alive. There were several appearances, one of them to Mary Magdalene.

...Mary stood outside the tomb crying. As she wept, she bent over to look into the tomb and saw two angels in white, seated where Jesus' body had been, one at the head and the other at the foot. They asked her, 'Woman, why are you crying?' 'They have taken my Lord away,' she said, 'and I don't know where they have put him.' At this, she turned round and saw Jesus standing there, but she did not realise that it was Jesus.

'Woman,' he said, 'why are you crying? Who is it you are looking for?' Thinking he was the gardener, she said, 'Sir, if you have carried him away, tell me where you have put him, and I will get him.' Jesus said to her, 'Mary.' She turned towards him and cried out in Aramaic,

'Rabboni!' (which means Teacher).

Jesus said, 'Do not hold on to me, for I have not yet returned to the Father. Go instead to my brothers and tell them, "I am returning to my Father and your Father, to my God and your God." ' Mary Magdalene went to the disciples with the news: 'I have seen the Lord!'

John 20:11–18 (NIV)

Mary Magdalene had gone to the place where Jesus was buried. And on the day after Tim's burial his father went up to the cemetery and knelt on the mound of earth that was his son's grave. He was devastated and utterly desolate. But he was praying, desperately wanting a word from God. He waited, almost without hope. Then it was as if God spoke to him in his heart—and asked him a question. 'Why seek ye the living among the dead?' Words from the Authorized Version of the Bible that Michael had known for years—and out of Luke's account of the mystery of the resurrection.

Now upon the first day of the week, very early in the morning, [the women] came unto the sepulchre, bringing the spices which they had prepared, and certain others with them. And they found the stone rolled away from the sepulchre. And they entered in, and found not the body of the Lord Jesus. And it came to pass, as they were much perplexed thereabout, behold, two men stood by them in shining garments: and as they were afraid, and bowed down their faces to the earth, they said unto them, Why seek ye the living among the dead? He is not here, but is risen: remember how he spake unto you when he was yet in Galilee. Saying, The Son of man must be delivered into the hands of sinful men, and be crucified, and the third day rise again. And they remembered his words.

Luke 24:1–8 (AV)

Michael has remembered those words too, since that day. So has Pam, because when she was at Tim's grave the words which God gave to her were, 'He is not here. He is risen.' The whole family are still mourning for Tim—and life will never be the same. But they believe they will see him again one day—and it makes a radical difference to their sorrow.

A reflection for Easter Day

Reflect on these sentences, several of which were on the inside cover of the Thanksgiving Service for Tim.

'I am the resurrection and the life; he who believes in me, though he die, yet shall he live, and whoever lives and believes in me shall never die.'

John 11:25–26 (RSV)

'... away from the body, and at home with the Lord.'

2 Corinthians 5:8 (RSV)

'Let not your hearts be troubled; believe in God, believe also in me. In my Father's house are many rooms; if it were not so, would I have told you that I go to prepare a place for you? And when I go and prepare a place for you, I will come again and will take you to myself, that where I am you may be also.'

John 14:1–3 (RSV)

'When they walk through the Valley of Weeping it will become a place of springs where pools of blessing and refreshment collect after rains!'

Psalm 84:6 (LB)

'I am sure that neither death, nor life, nor angels, nor principalities, nor things present, nor things to come, nor powers, nor height, nor depth, nor anything else in all creation, will be able to separate us from the love of God in Christ Jesus our Lord.

Romans 8:38–39 (RSV)

Finally, think about the words written to a member of his congregation by D.L. Moody, the great revivalist preacher who was born in 1837 and died in 1899.

'One of these mornings you will read in the paper, "Moody is dead!" But don't you believe it! On that morning I shall be more alive than I have ever been.'

Material for reflection and groups

Where do we go from here?

Many groups do not meet in Holy Week. But either this week or next week it would be good for the group to have a final meeting to ask, 'Where do we go from here?'

Ask each person to say if they got what they hoped for out of this group.

Then talk about the two-fold aim that we started with. To prepare the soil and to plan the planting. To pray that the inextinguishable blaze will burn more brightly—and to work out how to tell the good news to God's bad and beautiful world.

Make plans for the nourishment of your own spiritual life—as individuals and as a group.

Make plans to share the good news.

Finish by using this reflection—and let someone read it out slowly, with spaces for silence.

Imagine yourself as an earthenware candle-holder—filled and shining with the light and the glory of God ... The will of God for you (and for each one of us) is that we should radiate the light of the knowledge of God's glory in God's beloved world ... In your mind's eye, see Jesus washing his disciples' feet on the night before he died ... Then see Jesus on Good Friday, crucified—opening wide his arms for us on the cross. Then remember the glory of what happened on that first Easter morning ...

'Do everything without complaining or arguing, so that you may be innocent and pure as God's perfect children, who live in a world of corrupt and sinful people. You must shine among them like stars lighting up the sky as you offer them the message of life' (Philippians 2:14–15, GNB).